# "WIDE EYES AND BIG EARS"

## FRANK HARE

**MINERVA PRESS**
MONTREUX   LONDON   WASHINGTON

ISBN 1 85863 644 2




First Published 1996 by
MINERVA PRESS
1 Cromwell Place
London SW7 2JE




Printed in Great Britain by
B.W.D. Ltd., Northolt, Middlesex.

# "WIDE EYES AND BIG EARS"

*To my wife Chris*

All characters in this book are fictional,
and any resemblance to any person, living or dead,
is purely coincidental.

These are the observations of a young boy living in a northern town in England just after the Second World War. These reflections are recalled now as an adult and vividly portrayed with the innocence of the time now nearly fifty years ago. The humour and pathos are mixed to give descriptions of characters and events that were typical then.

# CHAPTER 1

Our street wasn't just any old street – it was OUR street. It was the backbone of the community – the main artery that bound us all together. During wars and hard times you could walk up the street and find friends who would share your problems, then promptly tell you about all the local scandal, so that by the time you got clear, you'd forgotten all about your own problems.

Very few people actually lived on the street, as it was made up of shops, two churches and a church hall. Everyone lived at right-angles to the street, down rows and rows of terraced houses, some facing directly onto the road, or if you were really classy, you had a front garden. But one thing they all had in common was a backyard and a back street. It was down these back alleys that all of us kids learned how to play football and cricket, but even more importantly, we experienced the fundamentals of the Facts of Life, either by sneaking up on unsuspecting courting couples, or when you got older by doing it yourself!

At the bottom of the street were the factories. Virtually every working person living in our neighbourhood got up each morning – went out of the door – turned left or right – depending on which side of the road you lived on – walked down the street for about seven or eight minutes and they were at work. It was all very orderly. Everyone knew the routine. A head would stick out of the barber's shop and call to a workmate,

"Hey chore – clock us in will yer? There's a queue in ere!" Why "chore" I never knew, but it made sense to everyone. But most of all, that little gesture made sure he received full pay whilst he was still having his hair cut, unbeknownst, of course, to the unsuspecting factory foreman.

With the men of the families that lived off the street all safely at work, the rest of the morning was spent by the wives doing the shopping, or as we younger kids would call it, "doin' the messages". Why? I simply don't know. But the daily gossip had begun in earnest. Up and down the street they went, to the butcher's, greengrocer's(3) newsagent's(2), grocer's, chemist, sweetshop(2), tobacconist's(4), pet shop, haberdasher's, post office, wet fish shop, baker, off licence, barber's, fish and chip shop, and above all, the 'Holy of Holies': the Co-op. All of these worthy establishments stretched for no more than three hundred yards from the top to the bottom of the street on each side.

With hardly any motorcars to be seen in this part of our town in 1945, local shops were the backbone of our neighbourhood and the essential centre for the sustenance of female life – GOSSIP! Where would they have been without it? The daily ritual of catching up on who had 'women's troubles', or was seen coming in late well after the pubs had shut.

"Rolling drunk he was".

"He never was!"

"He was yer know!"

All this HAD to take place because this was the North of England where every town had its in-built 'jungle telegraph'. Without it there would have been no communication and I am sure that the population of women would have curled up and died through the lack of it.

The street, therefore, was where it all happened – day in and day out – and especially in the butcher's, where, whilst waiting for the butcher to cut the required portion, the voices of doom spread the tales.

"Der yoo know, (essential pause) that bugger next to me was knocking hell oot of his Wife last night!"

"Never!" was the disbelieving reply.

"If he was mine, I'd kick him where the monkey keeps its nuts".

"Mind you, (pauses and looks around to make sure everyone else could hear), she's no angel. She was seen in the Three Crowns at the weekend knockin' em back with you know who from number 35".

"Well I never."

"It's right enough!"

"I saw her this mornin' – eyes black and blue. What a mess."

The butcher would come to the rescue, just as the shop was settling down to a round by round commentary: "That'll be two shillin's and six pence my dear, and will there be anything else today?"

With that, the two would leave the shop, deep in low-toned conversation whilst the rest of the queue could only guess at the sequel of ''er from next door and 'im from number 35'.

Summer time was the time of year when 'inter gossip' was as its height. Windows and doors were wide open and the daily bickerings could be heard several blocks away. But it was the sound of items being hurled across rooms that attracted the most attention, especially if it was followed by broken glass or crockery. The houses nearest the action would go into complete silence. "Mark my words, if I catch you playin' mothers and fathers again I'll skelp your arse" (interpretation:- skelp; to skin) "you dirty little bugger and wash your hands! I don't know where they've been!"


Now let me make it clear: life wasn't always full of physical activity but it certainly makes for a good story. Oh no, we had our fair share of exciting visual displays, like the girl at number 82 in our terrace, who regularly danced naked in front of her window making sure I could see her, until, one day, I assembled a gang of my mates to witness this spectacular from the seclusion of our woodshed. Everything was alright, with a lot of 'oohing and aahing' from the lads, until little Jimmy, in his anxiety to get a better viewing position, fell out of the shed and 'blew our cover'. That was the end of the strip shows.

Those long summer nights around 1946, artificially extended by double summertime, meant that bedtime was inevitably later than usual. This gave the neighbours a unique chance to meet outside each others' houses and pass the time recalling the war and the regular bombing raids. Our immediate neighbour, Tommy, had been the Air Raid warden who ran about the street like Corporal Jones in 'Dad's Army' shouting: "Don't panic!" One fine morning we could hear Tommy shouting up and down the street 'Don't panic, don't panic; it's all under control".

My Dad summoned me to the window to see Tommy scuttling up and down in front of the house directly opposite ours. Draped from the roof of the house was a parachute, shining all silken in the morning sun. This was great excitement indeed, but to Tommy this was WAR. It never occurred to me at the time, until Tommy drew it to everyone's attention, that this thing from the sky might have had a German on the end of it and a house-to-house search was undertaken immediately. Upstairs, downstairs, front gardens (for those with them) back yards, woodsheds coal houses – the lot, but to no avail. The arrival of an Army Officer in a truck put paid to the excitement by telling the assembled neighbourhood that the said parachute was indeed British and had probably fallen from a passing aircraft. What a disappointment! All that fuss for nothing. Well not quite; Tommy was given the job of guarding this object until a ladder could be found to get it down and safely back to its base. That really made his day, walking up and down the street shouting at all the kids "Keep back: this is Government property". The fact was, that the only people likely to pinch the damn thing were the women of the street, as it was made of pure silk and was something which they hadn't seen in years. It was taken away eventually much to everyone's disappointment, but especially to Tommy as it was the high point of the war, or at least HIS war.

Those seemingly endless summer evenings after the war, when the sun eventually set near midnight, encouraged us kids to play endless games of cricket and football just off the street and down miles of back streets, usually against your own back door. This was recanted by my friend Ronnie who had to read to the class in school his composition 'What I did over the weekend'. This resulted in an intricate monologue about how he played football against the backdoors of the neighbours' houses. This was too much for Mrs Puller, his teacher, as she stopped him halfway through this masterpiece and promptly administered three whacks of her bamboo cane across his hand for wilfully defacing other people's property. Poor Ronnie! He never could get it right. However he did have the last laugh on Mrs Puller when he signed professional forms for Sunderland Football Club a few years later.

Just off the street was the local dairy. It was part of a house just like any other house, with what looked like a brick garage tacked on at the side. I suppose nowadays it would have been shut down as a health hazard. It wasn't really a dairy with cows, but more like sub depot with the milk being delivered in huge churns which the milkman would take out in a hand pushed trolley with the churn swinging in the centre. Folks from the street would come out to the trolley when they heard the familiar cry 'MILKO'. Everything was measured in gills and poured from a tin plated scoop into each household's wide variety of jugs and bowls. When milk bottles eventually arrived after a few years when the post-war manufacturers could supply enough to keep the daily deliveries going, the time of delivering was halved. Alas, no more chit chat with the milkman and the neighbours. We definitely lost one of our greatest assets with the demise of the milk cart. But from a personal point of view, it was good news. This gave me access to a source of regular pocket money by helping the new style milkman. Teams of willing lads would scurry up and down the street delivering scores of bottles for six (old) pence a day. Up until this point in my life, I was set on being a Franciscan Monk, until one day all that changed, when I was delivering the daily pint to a rather gorgeous lady who was normally serviced (if you take my drift) by the milkman himself. Just as I was placing the bottle on the step, the lady of the house opened the door. She asked me to hand the bottle to her and, in doing so, a very large breast swung out from beneath her dressing gown. I was stunned and could only stare at this huge melon-shaped dollop which was directly at eye level and moving gently from side to side. Little did that innocent lady know that from that moment, my intended vocation as a Monk was over.

In the street, the church played a very big role in the lives of many of us. It was the vehicle for social contact at a different level than that found at the Co-op. For a start, it led us all to get to grips with the opposite sex in a big way, mainly by providing an excuse to be out late. Whilst our parents thought we were at Bible Class, we were actually at the church youth club dances, slinking around the parish hall dance floor, with arms legitimately around some hot little number who was only waiting to feel your hot breath on her neck. Well that was the idea anyway. As I viewed the assembled throng of neatly clad females just waiting to be asked to dance, my thoughts often strayed to my happy day on the milk round when that huge breast came my way and I wondered which of these girls might be game for a repeat performance in the shadow of the parish hall back street.

Ah what bliss it all was in those days! Church on a Sunday, then back to the parish hall on a hunting trip to grab what you could, when you could, and if she'd let you. My mother meanwhile needed to know no more than the fact that I was about my religious activities, which gave her and me much pleasure – especially me!

Well, that's a taste of our street. A not too special Northern town street which spawned a thousand stories. To an outsider, it didn't look much, but to all of us who lived there it was a place where we were at home, with friends and neighbours who knew each other and shared in each other's ups and downs. A simple scene really, but it was ours, and that made all the difference.

# CHAPTER 2

Our street was the providing link to all the houses that ran at right angles to it. Apart from the two churches, the parish hall and the school, the rest of our street was made up of shops of all types, which meant that shopping was only a few minutes away from your own front door at any time. So too was the place of work for most of the menfolk; just down the road a few blocks, and you were there. All very neat and tidy which as you can imagine meant that everybody knew everyone else's business.

This was fed through to us kids – just free from the war in 1946/47 – we were somehow liberated and able to express ourselves in public for the first time. So, as one war had ceased, gang wars began. Each gang had its own name: 'The King Street Gang', 'The Mills Road Gang', and most feared of all: 'THE BOMBER GANG'. This gang was made up from an area just next to the steelworks. A right tough lot they were too. Each had its own territory which was fiercely guarded and especially during those two weeks just before bonfire night.

Each gang had its own bonfire pitch which was jealously guarded against tribal raids from neighbouring gangs trying to pinch parts of it. Discarded furniture and household rubbish collected with great effort from doorstop collections was not to be lost to raiding tribes from a few streets away.

With sticks, poles, hammers, axes(!) and any other ad hoc weapon we could lay our hands on, we would fend off the raiders. Our 'look outs' would be perched high on the wooden fence which surrounded the local timber yard – known locally as 'amputation alley' as the workforce were constantly having their fingers cut off – they would whistle to the assembled gang that we were under attack. You could hear the yelling from the next street – they were coming! Up went the whistle from the 'look-out'.

"HERE THEY COME!" he screamed, scrambling down from his lofty position on top of the old railway sleepers that made up the timber yard fence and he was right: there were about twenty kids of all ages, dressed in all manner of get-ups to make themselves look aggressive, and believe me, they had succeeded. I was petrified. It was customary for me to position myself prominently at the rear of our gang, ready for that strategic withdrawal which usually came shortly after the invaders had turned the corner to face us. Well there are those born to be heroes and me. I knew my place and I stuck to it.

There was the traditional stand-off, with neither gang making any rash moves. Abuse was hurled back and forward with carefree abandon as it clearly was easier to overcome than a black eye or a sore head from a stray plank of wood launched from the rear of the opposing forces. Then, as usual in these affairs, somebody's mother would appear and spoil the whole thing by clearing the street single-handed by threatening to send for the police. This resulted in a casual withdrawal by both sides with a lot of mumblings and kicking of imaginary footballs as they retreated, heads down – until the next time.

At about this time, I discovered the Facts of Life in the flesh, as it were. I was a regular churchgoer and as a member of the choir and an altar boy, I was thought by the mothers of those much sought after girls, to be a good living chap, and a safe bet for their daughters. Ah well: that was their first mistake in personal assessment techniques. The church youth club provided the perfect cover for me and my mates to pursue our somewhat innocently evil ways. I was known as a 'very fast' one, probably because I was in a hurry to explore the incredible unseen parts I had never seen before, or something like that. I specialised in large girls. Well, it was a simple philosophy: 'If you want one, get a big un', and I usually did.

I suppose it was the fact that I brought out their motherly instincts, as I was a skinny kid and they always seemed so large. As for them sitting on my knee to canoodle, that was impossible, and inevitably we finished up with me sitting on HER knee.

Another method of measuring popularity with the girls down our street was if you were a good kisser. When the good Lord dished out the lips I came out with a top rating. This became embarrassing in the extreme when being invited to a party for a girl who lived nearby, I arrived to find that I was the ONLY BOY PRESENT! Jumping beansprouts! Escape was no use: the door was locked and I was about to be incarcerated in the kitchen pantry for over an hour with half a dozen panting girls eager for a kiss. I was eventually rescued by the girl's mother whose house it was. She couldn't believe what was going on and thought she was doing me a favour, but my gripe was that she didn't ask me, as I was quite happy as I recall. Needless to say, the news of this 'kissing slave' episode flashed around the street, resulting in many a pointed finger from those not so versed in the art of kissing as I was. "There 'ee goes – lushes lips laroo – give us a kiss pet". All very embarrassing for a youth only trying to explore the finer points of life, or something like that.


Now down our street we had several 'weirdos', one of whom we called 'Lurch'. Now 'Lurch' looked like a cross between Abraham Lincoln and Charles Dickens; very tall and thin with a wispy beard on the end of his chin. His face was always very white and he peered from behind thinly wired spectacles that always sat an inch from the end of his nose. He used to frighten all the kids to death simply by being there; creeping up on us unawares with a "Now boys – what's to do?" with a low-pitched voice so growling it always made us scream and run off. I suppose he was about sixty-five years old but looked a good hundred to us kids.

One of my favourite pastimes was avoiding him, as he always seemed to be picking on me, especially when it was football time in the back street near his house. Then one day during a kick-about I hoofed a ball over his wall and sneaked in to try and get it before 'Lurch' was onto me, but to no avail. Damn and drat, he jumped me in his backyard! After a few choice words threatening to call the police etc., I reminded him it was 'a free country' and I had 'a right to recover my property.' Well, that did it. He spent the next half an hour lecturing me on the laws of trespassing during which time my mates had cleared off home, bored stiff.

We thought that was the end of confrontations with 'Lurch', until one day, a stray boot thumped the ball over his wall again only to hear the sickening sound of breaking glass. We heard later that his kitchen window was smashed but we didn't stop to find out. We all had to fork out a week's pocket money each to repair it on the insistence of the local beat Bobby. Justice was swift in those days.

The local curate from the church was a single bloke called Carl. He dashed about the parish on a 1000cc Norton motor bike with a pair of goggles and a leather flying cap with flaps which did just that.

He was 'befriended' if you follow my drift, by most of the single lady parishioners who clearly felt that he was in need of care and attention and set about to provide it. This was all very neat and tidy until one day he was found with one of the lady flower arrangers in the vestry cupboard and was moved to another parish PDQ. I had my suspicions about him from the start when I was an altar server at the 7.15am Communion each Friday. When the service was finished, we had to clear up the wine chalices and Carl the curate had to swig up all the remaining wine himself, plus cleaning the chalices with a splash of wine from the flasks we would be holding. Splash – that was a laugh! Old Carl would hold your finger hard down on the wine flask and virtually fill the chalice full of wine and this was only 8am! We heard later that following an 'incident' at his new parish with the wife of the organist, he was sent to Africa as a missionary, minus the motorbike – to convert the local 'heathens' – but to what? The vicar, too, was a weird old soul. Later in life he developed a rather nasty twitch which had a very severe effect one morning service when a deputy organist, not familiar with this twitch – a rather violent movement of the head from side to side – caught a glimpse of the vicar in his mirror. Thinking that he was doing something wrong, he kept stopping and starting the hymns, much to the bewilderment of the congregation. The first hymn took about ten minutes to complete until the verger scrambled into the organ loft and tipped him off.

During a fund-raising effort, the vicar got all confused about who was for this particular scheme and who wasn't and summarised it as follows;

"One lady here tonight with whom I have been on intimate terms for many years is FOR the scheme, whilst her daughter is against it. I have, however, only been intimate with the daughter for the first time this evening." You could have heard a pin drop.

Shortly afterwards the Vicar made a mildly humorous joke and the roof nearly went off.

Now lower down our street was the 'demon barber' Cedric. Now Cedric was of a rather peculiar gender – nobody knew what it was!

Was it man, woman, a mixture of both? God only knew! I honestly believe that Cedric didn't either. He had his hair brushed over his balding head and flicked up on the other side. Some days his hair was blue and on other days it was – wait for it – STRAWBERRY BLOND! Yet here he was accepted by this working class post-war community for most of his life and he must have been sixty if he was a day.

The return of the male hair cut with a ridge round the head recently, reminded me of Cedric – he invented it. Not as you would think by using models, but usually by accident. One look in the mirror before you left his shop was all the evidence that you needed to convince yourself that you would be spending the next two weeks indoors until it grew again. Add to this the guarantee that when shaving your sideburns he would almost always cut you with the open razor, sending you home with white blotches on your face from those blood stopping stiptic pencils he had at the ready. Some days, when Cedric stood outside his shop in his white overall, it was difficult to determine whether he had more blood on it than the butcher two doors up the street.

His range of stories was the real reason why we all put up with this palaver. He had the full range, from the innocent to the downright filthy. Lowering his voice when coming to the juicy bits, so that we young guns couldn't hear the punch lines, he entertained the male population of the neighbourhood for over thirty years. It was not unknown for a trip to the barber's to take up to two hours, as men would often stay behind to hear more of Cedric's best stories, whilst he 'minced' around the shop with his cracked high-pitched voice, rattling them off before his captive and often bleeding audience. The fact was that he was a devoted son to his ageing mother, who lived above the barber's shop. They had lived together since his father was killed in the First World War, leaving them without a penny. Cedric then took to the barber's trade out of sheer necessity to support his Mother and make ends meet. He had done a stint on the stage, so he said. But as what? It definitely wasn't a walk-on part with that style of his. We all had our suspicions, but never let on. Sadly, when his Mother eventually went to that 'big barber's shop in the sky', he closed his shop one night and failed to open the next morning. They found him in the chair with a bottle of aspirins by his side, dead and gone. It was all too much for him: his Mother was his life and that was all he had. When she went, he went too. All very tragic.

At his funeral, the church was packed to capacity and at his request, they sang the hymn 'O sacred head surrounded' so that all his former customers could remember his antics with the open razor as the third line goes: 'O bleeding head so wounded'.

Well that's another little extract from 'Our Street'. Not just any old street – as it was OUR street where WE lived and none the worse for that.

# CHAPTER 3

"Oh dear, oh dear, whatever next" came the cry from one older resident of our street. This anguished comment was made after seeing Margie at play again. Now Margie was about twenty years of age, very tall dark and very 'playful', if you follow the drift. In short, she liked the boys – not any particular boy, just ANY BOY, or man for that matter. Alas, she was a 'few cards short of a full pack', which meant she was fair game for any lusting youth who happened to be in the area.

Her favourite pitch was in the sand dunes at the beach, which was half an hour's walk away from our street along the sea front. But if any particular suitor was in a hurry, then she made do with the rear alley at the back of her house. The particular day which gave rise to the dismay shown by the aged resident, was as a result of Margie cavorting with this active youth against the back street wall whilst eating fish and chips at the same time! I overheard a passing youth say it was a waste of good fish and chips.

Alas Margie came to a sticky end, as she was last seen – after a short absence – pushing a pram in the park at the far side of town, containing the 'fruits of her indiscretions' as the church caretaker was overheard saying. Poor Margie!

Whilst thinking of the church caretaker, it reminds me that he was very prone to a drop of the 'hard stuff', which more than complimented the curate at the time, whose heavy-handed dealings with the communion wine has been mentioned earlier in these tales from our street.

The caretaker wasn't difficult to identify in this regard, as his red and very pitted nose seemed to precede him by a clear margin when walking towards you. He was known to have a wide variety of booze strategically secreted in all manner of places within the bounds of the church and the nearby church hall, both being located in our street and less than a hundred yards apart.

During a big effort by the regular churchgoers to spring clean the church prior to Easter, it was necessary to remove the vestry grandfather clock which had been donated years before by some faithful soul. The delicate head was removed first by the local undertaker who was a dab hand at clocks. But in the absence of the caretaker who was otherwise occupied, the main body of the clock was lifted up by a sturdy youth, only to be struck on the foot by a full bottle of gin which fell out of the case. Clearly, the caretaker had forgotten all about it, but sadly for him, it smashed onto the vestry floor and he hadn't the gall to lay claim to it, and merely fetched a pan and brush to clear up the mess.

As it was a wooden blocked floor, the place smelt of gin for weeks afterwards, much to the annoyance of the vicar – who was teetotaller – when it suited him.

At the top of our street and opposite the church, was the confectioner's, or as we kids called it, the sweet shop. It was owned by an ex-war hero who had been seriously injured, which had resulted in a wooden leg. I suppose we would say 'artificial leg' nowadays but you can take it from me it was wooden, as a peculiar incident revealed.

It was just before Easter, about 1949, with rationing still in force and chocolate hard to come by in any quantity. The sweet shop owner, Fred, was trying his best to interest the public with a display of what chocolate he had in his shop window. To get into this window required a bit of climb through a sliding partition between us kids and the display.

This display was all too much for a scruffy kid called Rutter, who was eyeing up the bars on the meagre shelves. When Fred was adjusting the window one day, Rutter, realising that Fred couldn't move too quickly, proceeded to sneak a hand around the partition and snaffle the nearest bar of that succulent product when Fred spotted him.

With a quick turn he just missed grabbing Rutter by the arm, but succeeded in tumbling backwards out of the window and onto the shop floor. Needless to say Rutter was off at a rate of knots.

Fred meanwhile had got to his feet and was about to give chase when, without warning he crashed to the floor again. On observing the scene it was clear why – Fred was minus one leg and was going nowhere! The leg however was clearly visible on the shop floor and I can confirm – it was DEFINITELY made of wood.


Most parents down and around our street cursed the day that some whizz kid introduced stink bombs to the local shops.

Most of the time, these were being aimed at kids from one of the many street gangs that roamed the area, with the exception of one memorable evening. It was during one of those balmy long double summertime evenings just after the war, when being outside was essential, as it was so humid.

Close by our street was a privately owned meeting room called the 'Glass Hall' by the locals as the three sides were entirely made of a glass. It was really a lean-to shed which backed onto the local privately owned butcher's shop and was mostly used as a whist drive venue for the locals. You could see clearly into the room which held I suppose fifty or sixty card-playing addicts two nights a week.

One local youth who rejoiced in the name of 'Orry' – short for Horace (his parents clearly had a keen sense of humour), was feeling particularly restless during one of these humid evenings and got very upset when he was constantly being chased from the front of the Glass Hall, which, on this occasion had all the front doors and windows wide open. He vowed to have his revenge and earlier that day, he had swapped a large 'gobstopper' (a large sweet to new readers) for – yes, you've guessed it – a stink bomb!

Those dreaded weapons could reek throughout a building for days with a pungent and sickening smell of rotten eggs. Orry was intent on doing his worst to get his revenge on the hall superintendent who clearly had it in for him. With a carefully aimed lob – Orry being a keen cricketer – the stink bomb landed smack in the middle of the assembled throng of card players.

The smell was horrific and despite the efforts of the superintendent to kick the object out of the hall, it was too late. A stampede ensued, with the old dears rushing for the open glass door and fresh air, choking as they went cursing and swearing. "Wait till I get my hands on that little bugger!" shouted the superintendent. But his death-wish fell on deaf ears, as Orry was long gone and the whist drive ended in chaos with tables and chairs overturned in the rush to get out.

It turned out that Orry was the subject of a visit from the local 'Plod' who gave him a dressing down in the school assembly, much to everyone's amusement except Orry who was given a punishment by the Headmaster – sweeping out the Glass Hall for the next two weeks with every kid in the street looking in. Boy was he mad! The stink bomb craze fizzled out at about the same time, much to the relief of the card playing fraternity.

For the record, Orry became a Minor Counties cricketer several years later. His stink bomb throwing episode was not entirely in vain, it seems.


The local primary school in our street kept its inmates working there until they were eleven, with the 'clever dicks' going to the Grammar and Technical schools if they hurdled the dreaded eleven plus exam. The whole world it seemed to us kids, was geared to passing this damned exam, with parents getting paranoid the nearer the day came. Those kids faced with this trauma were tested and better tested to gear up their brainwaves with all sorts of facts that might come in handy on the big day. This included initiative tests, one of which was tried once and only once for reasons that will become all too apparent.

The top class were given a special task of sampling public opinion on various topics of their choosing. Now the idea was that each pupil would go into the street and ask various questions of the general public on a particular topic and compile simple statistics to be marked by the teacher.

Now this sounded fine, but it took no account of those bright sparks out for a lark who were out to do mischief come what may. Apart from the usual wheeze of nipping behind the loos and having a drag on a fag, the system overlooked Wacker Simpson – the name coming from his Liverpudlian background and accompanying accent. Wacker was in short, outside the system altogether, the proverbial cheeky chappie with a ready-made answer for most occasions. Now this early answer to market research was right up Wacker's street and outside too! It was like liberating the chimps at the zoo and making them the management for the day. The school must have been crazy letting Wacker anywhere the general public with a board pencil and paper, asking them anything HE liked.

Being advanced for his age, Wacker went to town as we learned later, with a unique line of questioning to the passing female public. Yes – it was specifically aimed at women, with disastrous results, the details of which we didn't hear about until Wacker came back to school following his suspension. Apparently he thought it a good idea to ask those unsuspecting ladies who crossed his path about the modern style of women's bras. Followed quickly by a punchy first question before they could draw breath of: "—and do you suffer from nipple ripple Madame?" His feet didn't touch the ground once the Headmaster heard about it and out he went! Needless to say he was the school hero on his return and renamed 'Nipple Wacker' from that day onwards.

The facts are, that on reflection all these years later, we had down and around our street more than our fair share of nutcases, eccentrics and plain screwballs. This included the one and only Wilf, a resident bachelor who lived just behind the church with his aged mother.

Now, Wilf's only claim to fame was that he was profoundly forgetful to the point of being on occasions, downright dangerous. He simply could not remember anything of importance despite the fact that he was reasonably educated and had a doting Mother who kept him on the straight and narrow most of the time.

The stories are many about his antics, most of which centred around the period he was in the Home Guard. He was walking one day to the drill hall in full uniform one evening in the pouring rain when he was overtaken by his platoon Sergeant Major. Instead of wearing the usual army style cape, Wilf was carrying an umbrella! This was bad enough for a man whom the Country relied on in those desperate days to fend off the encroaching enemy, but instead of his rifle that he should have been carrying, he had three empty milk bottles under his arm. He had forgotten to put them at the front door on leaving home and had left his rifle there in the milk crate instead! The Sergeant wasn't too pleased!

There are so many stories about Wilf that you could fill a book, but one that comes to mind as exceptional, was when he went to see the local football team play in the third round of the cup against Chelsea from the first division. With not too much being expected of the team from the Third Division North, the crowd was just waiting for the visitors to crack in half a dozen, but it wasn't to be.

Wilf as usual arrived too late for a good position and found himself at the back of the terrace, which was really a mud heap with a few steps which stopped halfway up the bank. This didn't suit Wilf, who spied a table abandoned by the turnstile when the gates were closed. He scurried down the bank and hauled it up the bank and proudly stood on it, which made him some three feet taller than everyone else. This was fine until the local team scored. The crowd went mad - jumping up and down which needless to say included Wilf. But as usual he got it wrong with the result that the table and Wilf went flying down the back of the embankment and into the ice-cream trolley, spreading wafers and cornets in all directions, including Mr Polluci the Italian ice-cream man who went berserk. He made Wilf pay for the damage at a pound a week. This really upset Wilf, as he was allergic to ice-cream!

Well that's the latest from our street – not just any old street – but our street – and we loved it.

# CHAPTER 4

Whilst our street did not have its own chapel of rest, we did have our resident undertaker who was mostly to be found around the church as he doubled as an altar server and rejoiced in the name of Fred Cox. He was better known as 'Cox the Box'.

Now, Cox was to say the least a practical joker, which was rather disconcerting when you consider his vocation. You never quite knew what he was up to, as many an altar boy would find out to his detriment and usually without warning.

One unsuspecting youth, who was at his first communion as an altar server alongside Cox, was handed a flask containing the wine during the service. His job was to help the vicar during the filling of the chalices. Unknown to the youth, Cox had swapped the wine for a very strong local beer and as he was pouring it into the chalice it frothed up, cascading over the side with the youth hurriedly trying to scoop it back in with his hand. Cox to his credit, once he had had his giggle, stepped in with the proper wine and all was well.

Needless to say, his reputation was widespread and it was only a matter of time before one of his 'victims' had his revenge. One of Cox's assistants in the funeral parlour who was regularly subjected to these pranks, laid on a daring jape on the unsuspecting Cox right in his own back parlour.

Cox (never Coxey for the record) always insisted on being present when the grieving mourners were saying their fond farewells prior to the securing of the coffin lid which he personally placed in position. On one such occasion, his assistant struck. Cox had ushered the mourners back into the parlour having paid their respects to the departed, and proceeded to place the lid in position. To his horror his assistant had swapped the plate bearing the name of the deceased and replaced it with a specially engraved one with

Cox's name on it. A good deal of scurrying around and somewhat blasphemous language ensued to correct the situation, without the knowledge of the funeral party, but to the sniggering delight of Cox's assistant who couldn't wait to pass the word around our street. Alas, it didn't cure Cox, but it stopped his antics for a while.


During the war, the Luftwaffe made a pinpoint hit on our local swimming baths which put it out of action for several years. When fully rebuilt, it formed the centre of much social activity until the novelty wore off, resulting in the early morning sessions being almost empty. Rod, (that wasn't his real name) the local apprentice plumber, found these early morning sessions very conducive to his courting strategy with one of the local maidens out of the local greengrocer's shop.

Rod was having trouble with the young lady's mother who was constantly breaking up their clinches on the front doorstep and usually at the vital moment. So he arranged to meet the young lady (a distinct misnomer if you follow my drift) at the opening of the swimming baths at about seven in the morning. With nobody around, the pair of them could frolic about in the changing rooms to their heart's content, with the overbearing mother still tucked up in bed and no doubt dreaming of her daughter enjoying her early morning exercises. How right she was!

Rod of course was full of himself about this coup over 'the old dragon', couldn't keep his mouth shut and let this slip to one of his mates. Yes, you've guessed it, catastrophe loomed large for Rod (often prefixed with the word 'hot' by his mates – I can't think why) when two other apprentices from the same firm slipped into the swimming baths without Rod and his girlfriend knowing. With their usual morning 'exercises' well underway, one of the apprentices slid their swimming gear from under the cubicle partition and the other removed their clothes from their locker and replaced them in another.

When the two love birds were due to finish off the proceedings with a dip in the pool to at least look the part for the unsuspecting mother, they discovered the dreadful truth! It took some time to summon the attendant to convince him of their predicament, which led to 'the word' getting out to Rod's mates about the naked truth of his early morning 'dips'!

Schoolboy antics when you are a schoolboy seemed quite natural at the time, but with the benefit of hindsight, as an adult, you look back with horror at what one got up to. Even the relative sanctuary of the local church choir gave rise to some of these events. It was the custom for all new starters in the choir to undergo an 'initiation ceremony' totally unknown to the choirmaster – although I am sure that he had his suspicions that something was afoot, but was not sure what.

The severity of the 'ceremony' really depended on the boy in question and how well he was standing up to it.

On one occasion, a rather fat boy (always a target for more than the average treatment) had joined the choir from a neighbouring church and had previously been the sworn enemy of the head boy of our lot. He could hardly wait for the choir practice to end to get his hands on the poor unsuspecting little fat boy.

The first torture was to force the fat boy to eat the moss off the gravestones in the churchyard. Now eating moss at any time was bad enough – but off the gravestones! The boy promptly threw up and started whingeing: never a good idea in front of boys baying for his demise. This prompted the head boy to bring the proceedings to an end by pushing the fat boy down the steps of the church boiler room which was pitch black, resulting in the poor wretch twisting his ankle and having to be helped out and carried home, with a cock and bull story that he'd fallen by accident. Eventually the boy blubbed to his doting mother the whole truth, citing the head boy as the architect of the proceedings. The choirmaster at the insistence of the vicar, set a punishment for the head boy. He was to be confined during the next Sunday service, to rear of the organ and loft where he was forced to hand pump the organ bellows. Now this practice had ceased some years earlier when the bellows had been fitted with an electric pump, the idea being that the bellows were filled by means of a large wheel which was turned constantly when the organist was playing. The head boy was not at all chuffed with this demeaning task and had the last laugh. Any failure to turn the wheel – which was about four feet in diameter – resulted in no wind for the pipes and no music. The head boy waited his moment to pounce. During the last hymn, rather than stopping turning the wheel, he varied the rate of turning with the result that the tune was sinking and rising through the hymn. The vicar was furious and ordered the verger to clamber into the organ loft and snatch the wheel and restore the final hymn to a successful end. The head boy, as his excuse, said that he was feeling sick in the organ loft and couldn't continue. This didn't wash with the choirmaster who sacked him. The now former head boy had the last laugh however, by sneaking back into the church vestry and puncturing the bellows of the harmonium which was used for rehearsals, which put paid to that activity for a few weeks until it could be repaired.

Thinking of repairs reminds me that next to the ice-cream parlour down our street was the bicycle repair shop, which was run by a man and his wife named Hoggett. Now the Hoggetts, which was near enough to being called 'Sprockets' or 'Sprock' for short were dour people. Hardly ever raising a smile, they went about their business of mending bikes, and as a sideline recharging radio accumulators which were an old fashioned form of battery for those houses with no electricity in those days. Hard to imagine as it is today, but there really were such houses which relied solely on solid fuel or gas.

The 'Sprocks' had cornered the market and they knew it, resulting in them purposely delaying the recharging of the batteries of those they did not approve of viz anybody who wasn't a Mormon as they were. This as you can imagine, these few years after the war, eliminated 99.9% of the neighbourhood. In short, they hated everybody and everybody hated them. It was nothing new to hear old 'Sprock' laying the law down outside his shop to an undeserving customer, about the social morals of the people in and around our street. Standing there as usual, absolutely filthy – and that went for him AND his wife – raging about the behaviour of the local kids. Needless to say, they hadn't any of their own. The 'Sprocks' were constantly arguing with virtually every customer about their level of charges with the net effect that if you could fix your own bike you did to avoid going anywhere near them.

Needless to say, they went too far with young Orry, mentioned earlier in this missive, who took exception to a bill presented to him for a small repair to his front wheel. On realising that Orry was not about to pay, 'Sprock' confiscated Orry's bike. Oh dear me! Now Orry's Dad was not a man to be mucked about with and on hearing about 'Sprocks' action, promptly went to the shop and confronted him. After a heated argument, which was much enjoyed by the rest of the street, resulted in 'Sprock' being hurled across a row of bikes, and Orry and his Dad leaving with their machine and no payment made at all.

It must be something of a very unusual coincidence that the next shop but one down our street from the sweet shop (the confectioner to new readers) owned by a man with one leg, was the chemist shop run by a pharmacist with one arm. The remnants of the last war were only too plain to see. The pharmacist (we all called him the chemist) had a false arm in the shape of a hook which was in two pieces. By some means or other, these hooks could part, enabling the pharmacist to grip almost anything which wasn't too wide. It will not surprise anyone that the pharmacist was duly nick-named 'Captain Hook' or just 'Hooky' for short.

Now 'Hooky' had a way with the womenfolk of the area around our street which I suppose had something to with his hooked arm which as lads, came as something of a shock, as we had no conception of how he could manage to get to grips with such things (if you follow my meaning).

As a result of this weakness in his character, he was always hiring shop assistants of a somewhat easy virtue, who did not regard his hooked hand as a deterrent, but more of an incentive if not a little kinky.

Regrettably these 'ladies' were all too often rather loud of speech, which meant that if you wished to purchase anything of a rather 'delicate' nature, which required some form of description, you could find yourself in an acutely embarrassing situation, being faced with this loud-mouthed female telling your intimate details to all of the other shoppers plus half of the street who were within earshot.

Alas, it befell me to do such an errand for my old grandfather, who was having trouble with piles and required more suppositories, and who sent me to the chemist for them. I hovered outside the shop until I was sure the pharmacist was on his own, to get in and out without being overheard by anyone else – especially his assistant! I made my move. There he was – all alone. Great! I thought.

Then tragedy struck – the phone rang. He was summoned to the rear of the shop and I was eyeball to eyeball with his dreaded assistant! Nightmare of nightmares. I managed to splutter out the trade name of the suppositories but it was inaudible. Even more panic – another customer came into the shop. I was bright red and wished the ground would swallow me up. Oh God! She then asked me to describe the dreaded things! I thought the torture would never end. I explained as best I could what they were used for to the woman and to my horror she bawled out to the pharmacist at the rear of the shop:

"This kid wants some sort of pill that you stuff up your bum to stop piles!". By now my face was on fire. I paid for the damn things and ran out of the shop vowing never to enter there again.

That was the trouble with our street – secrets were well nigh impossible to keep. My only thought was, as I ran to my grandfather's house, that everybody would think the damn things were for me!

# CHAPTER 5

The headmaster of the local school down our street was known as 'Bruiser', which described very well the results of his punishment meted out to his pupils over many years – usually with his stick made from a whacky sort of cane. Now 'Bruiser', although he had been headmaster for over twenty years had never had the privilege or convenience of a telephone at the school. It is difficult to comprehend this now in this age of telecommunications, but it was true nevertheless. This meant he could be seen trekking up and down our street several times a day to the public phone box which was situated a couple of hundred yards from the school. Whilst this may have given him a break from his usual routine in his office, it could be very inconvenient and on one occasion almost fatal.

On one such occasion during a very hot spell of weather one summer, the school doors and windows were left wide open to ventilate the place. Alas, this corresponded with a breeze which kept closing the doors, often with a bang. The inevitable happened – a loud bang – a shrill scream shot through the school. Some unsuspecting child had left his fingers in the door jam as it slammed shut, resulting in three severed fingers and a lot of pain. The child was bleeding freely and a tight bandage was applied as an immediate first aid, but with the absence of a telephone, panic set in. Fortunately the local vicar was passing and offered a lift in his car (one of the very few around our street at that time) to the hospital.

Whilst nothing in those days could be done for the child's fingers, by something of a miracle, a telephone was hastily installed. This was to be for the exclusive use of the headmaster and was promptly placed in box specially made for it by the school caretaker. Just to defy logic a little further, it was of little use in emergencies when the Headmaster was absent from his office as he had the only key! A crazy old world indeed.


It is difficult to believe now that during this period just after World war Two, there were some ten cinemas within walking distance of our street. All showed twice nightly films with a 'B' movie, a main feature film, the news and the obligatory cartoon or one of those boring travelogue films. The audiences would get very restless during those travelogue films which were mainly nature programmes from North America or Canada. Often certain sections of the local youths would start a slow hand-clap or jeer at bears catching fish in a fast-flowing river. This would infuriate one manager known locally as Uncle wart. His real name was Walter, but he had an unfortunate wart-like spot on his nose, which made him quite conspicuous in any crowd. Uncle wart always wore a smart dinner jacket often with non matching trousers even when queuing at the butchers. He simply had to keep up his appearance come what may. Rowdy youths were his speciality as he would yank them from their seats and frog-march them up the aisles, through the swing doors and into the street. However, his eyesight wasn't too good in the darkened cinema and on one occasion this proved to be his downfall. He had given the obligatory warning with a flash of his torch to a certain section of noisy youths which had no effect as they were all bored stiff with the travelogue and wanted the James Cagney film on instead. Unfortunately, Uncle wart singled out a a red-headed boy the first time and on his return, having failed to stop the jeering, pulled the red-headed boy out of his seat, and proceeded to throw him out. wart then returned to the same noisy area for a public warning to the rest of the gang regarding their future conduct when to his utter amazement, the red-headed boy was back in his seat.

Protesting furiously that he was innocent of all charges, the boy was led up the aisle, through the swing doors and into the street. At this point, Uncle wart nearly had heart failure as there outside was the boy he had thrown out earlier. He too was red-headed – yes you've guessed they were identical twins! In his fluster, and trying to half apologise for his mistake, he couldn't decipher who was who. The twins realising this, refused to own-up with the result that Uncle wart let them both back in rather than refund the money to the wrong twin.

By this time, James Cagney was well underway, shooting and punching and all was forgotten.


Now just off our street was a smart little terrace of five houses, the central one being owned by a part Irish, part Belgian and part English family noted for their ability to start a fight at the drop of a hat. This propensity would often manifest itself on New Year's Eve, when all the menfolk had had a whack of ale at the local boozer, prior to the chimes of Big Ben at midnight.

On one such occasion at about half an hour before the chimes, an argument broke out between the various factions as to who did what during the war. The first punch was thrown within minutes. Crash, bang wallop! There was furniture everywhere. The next door neighbours were sent for to try to break it up, but to no avail. Each in turn would return home to report on the progress – have a drink – then proceed back to the fracas and attempt to pull the participants apart.

This went on for over half an hour, and above the clatter, the chimes of Big Ben heralding in the New Year, could be heard and the Archbishop of Canterbury on the radio praying for lasting peace throughout the world. Alas, his message hadn't reach these parts just off our street as the fight continued unabated. That was until an almighty crash stopped the proceedings dead.

The giant aspidistra that stood in the front window and which was a family heirloom handed down through at least one generation, went crashing through the window and into the street. All hostilities stopped! The three main participants ran into street and gathered up the broken vase and the remnants of the plant and carefully carried it back into the house. There they were confronted by the ageing grandfather of the family just finishing off the second chorus of 'Auld Lang Syne'. Traditions, it seems, prevail no matter what. My grandmother, who lived nearby, was heard to comment: "They think more of that bloody plant than they do of each other". She was right too.

Most towns during the war, established that great civic amenity 'The British Restaurant' – later to be renamed: 'The Civic Restaurant', presumably to help everyone forget the standard of meals it dished out. Our British Restaurant was a short walk from our street in the main shopping area and adjoined the indoor market. It always reminded me of aircraft hanger, with its ornate cast iron roof structure. The wooden tables and chairs spread around the concrete floor always meant that it was a bit chilly even in high summer.

It provided inexpensive meals at a time of rationing to anyone who cared to attend which was a Godsend to those with no one to cook for them or just plain lonely and, of course, hungry. It also provided work for armies of ladies who could cook, serve up and wash up usually at great speed, as the restaurant only provided meals from 12 noon to 2 pm and usually it was packed with several hundred people each day except Sundays.

It was a prerequisite for such an establishment to have a strong manager who could drive the staff on with as little fuss as possible and get the customers in and out in the shortest time. Our British Restaurant had just the person – Mrs Amy Peobody.

Mrs P, as she was known, had the build of an all-star wrestler and voice that could turn tea cakes into stone, which is what they normally tasted like at the BR. There was a rumour going around that at one time that she doubled for the air raid siren during the war when it broke down. She was certainly up to it.

Whilst I am absolutely positive that she got the work done in double quick time, she made many enemies en route. The staff were constantly grumbling about her – never to her face of course, as that would have been 'curtains' for such treachery and a sacking without hesitation. There was no employment protection in those days, simply a queue of people waiting to take up the vacancy.

Customers also often got the thick end of her tongue, especially slow movers at the counter, as it was all self-service. Even local school teachers were to be found at lunch time at the BR, which didn't say much for the school meals to which they were entitled. They too were whipped into line by the dreaded Mrs P who would stride up and down behind the servers at the counter issuing verbal assaults to all and sundry who came within earshot, which included almost everybody within a half mile radius of the restaurant.

It wasn't until Mrs P took on a rather belligerent young woman called Maudie, that anyone had dared challenge her or even question one of her decisions. Now Maudie simply couldn't live without a regular fag. So she set about to monitor Mrs P's movements in order to get a quick drag in when she wasn't looking.

Being a simple soul, Maudie hadn't latched onto the fact, that even if Mrs P hadn't seen her, she could certainly smell the resulting smoke. The boom was lowered one day with the ultimatum that whoever it was who was smoking would be 'hung drawn and quartered' and sent promptly down the road for their pains. As predicted, Maudie paid no heed to this and was caught having a quick drag behind the refuse bins outside the back door of the restaurant. Mrs P marched Maudie straight to the locker room and out she went straight to the nearest exit. But one thing Maudie didn't like was being pushed around by anybody, including Mrs P and on her way out she pushed over a whole vat of cold custard all over the floor and Mrs P's shoes. Mrs P grabbed Maudie by the collar and pushed her into the office and locked the door and sent for the police.

She was eventually bound over to keep the peace at the local magistrates court, much to Mrs P's disgust, especially as the report in the local newspaper had reported Maudie calling Mrs P 'a dragon', with the headline: 'Dragon Slayed by Custard.'

The British Restaurant eventually closed when its clientele reduced to a few 'down and outs' some years later. But it served its purpose by filling a gap brought about by hard times. I can still smell the gravy and mashed potato – they're still my favourite.

# CHAPTER 6

Not far from our street along the beach road was one of two local golf courses. At that time, just after the war with most things very scarce, the idea of being able to afford the fees for such pursuits was far from most peoples' minds, especially the folk down our street. However, this did not stop the local lads from fielding balls that had been lost by those lucky enough to be members of the club. Normally the lads would hover around the edge of the fairways keeping a keen eye open for someone who had lost a ball and promptly offering to join in the hunt, usually for an sixpenny piece reward if the mission was successful.

There were those of course who pocketed the ball when found and seeing the golfer disappearing into the distance made off with it and later offered to sell it to another golfer for a good profit.

Needless to say, these lads became well known at the course and they in turn knew the members. It wasn't until one fine mid-week day during the school holidays that two of these regular lads were as usual hunting for lost balls as the course was almost empty.

Around the ninth hole were a number of redundant bunkers which had been filled in and allowed to grass over. As the lads came to the top of one of these bunkers to their utter amazement they stumbled upon two partly clothed women lying down making love! The lads being so shocked at these goings on – which they had only heard about in dodgy magazines and decades before gay liberation – scurried back to the club house to identify the two women as they had failed to do so at the time due to their hasty retreat.

They waited alas in vain. No women of that description were to be seen. No doubt the two had left the course by another exit. This as you can well imagine, became the talk of the course when the lads let the 'cat out of the bag' with their mates. From that moment onwards and for weeks to come, every lad who frequented the course, was on the look out for these women with great enthusiasm and excitement, but to no avail: it was the one and only such 'performance', much to the regret of the lads who were hoping to improve their carnal knowledge a bit further – always a worthy pursuit.

Just off our street was the local timber yard run by an autocratic brute called Sid. Now Sid ran this timber yard with an 'iron rod' which basically meant that if you didn't pull your weight, you were out.

The yard was really the refuge for those who were at the bottom of the employment pile and couldn't find a job anywhere else. It attracted, as you can imagine, a motley crew who were to be seen scurrying back and forth from the huge piles of timber to the circular and vertical saws which made such a racket. They were enough to keep most people not just awake, but slightly disorientated with the constant high pitched whining throughout the working day.

The dreaded Sid would march up and down cracking his verbal 'whip' to all and sundry. It was hardly surprising that accidents featured highly in amongst this mayhem and on a regular basis. Severed fingers were very common. The poor unfortunate workers who injured themselves were usually rushed by taxi, hired by Sid, to the hospital which was only a five minute ride after the initial somewhat crude first aid had been administered by Sid himself. It was always felt that he laid on taxis to persuade the work force that he was the model employer, when in fact he was only trying to keep the workers from reporting him to the factory inspector.

As can be well imagined, the blokes were always on the look out for ways of getting back at Sid and one day the opportunity came to the least likely person as 'Martin the Mole'. Why the 'Mole'? Quite simple really; he had a long nose, beady eyes with spectacles and was dead ringer of Mole in The Wind in the Willows. He walked very sheepishly looking from side to side as if he was about to be pounced on at any minute by some alien. Not the sort of guy to take on the dreaded Sid you would have thought, but that was exactly what happened!

Sid always brought a sandwich lunch to work every day and stored it in his makeshift cupboard when he arrived each morning at 7.30am.

Poor old Martin had been getting some 'stick' from Sid for some days and this culminated in Martin falling down and spraining his ankle, which annoyed Sid in the extreme. He could probably see another taxi fare coming his way.

But rather than go sick and probably lose his job, Martin struggled on, volunteering to make the tea for all the blokes in the yard and generally tidying around. He made up an ad hoc crutch from two pieces of scrap wood and hobbled about, scurrying about the place at a pace faster than he normally did when he was fully fit. But he was determined to pull a stunt on Sid and the moment eventually came. This timber yard covered quite an area bounded by a fence made of old railway sleepers which was generally overrun with rats and mice , much to the annoyance of the neighbours whose cats were always on overtime keeping the vermin under control. Martin saw his chance. It wasn't until one lunchtime when the God Almighty scream of screams came from Sid's tumbledown apology for an office. He came out, choking, spitting and cursing. Having started to eat his sandwich, he failed to notice that it had been half eaten by a mouse which had been slipped into his lunch box by Martin, during his tea making duties.

Sid went crazy. He demand to know who had done this, storming around the yard picking up bits of wood and hurling them at anyone daft enough to be in his vicinity. Martin meanwhile went about his duties looking over his glasses at anything but Sid. Despite interrogating all and sundry, nobody split on Martin and Sid was left to wonder what other tricks were coming his way, resulting in a quelling of his temper for a few weeks. That was until the factory inspector inevitably called and placed a closure notice on the yard, pending a very costly safety programme which was to be put in hand which nearly sent Sid 'up the pole'. It wasn't the new safety gear that got him down, he admitted later, it was all those taxi fares that he had wasted over the years. What a berk! Sid eventually got his just rewards. The timber yard was burned to the ground about a year later. Sid failed again to find out how it happened, but the shock was too much this time. He died of a heart attack shortly afterwards. The yard never reopened which made most of the cats in the area redundant and the local taxi business very short of work.

At that time just after the war, we kids had all sorts of crazes to occupy our time, in those days before television and video games. It was usually something that came and went in a few weeks.

One such craze was the cobbling up of a wooden catapult which looked like gun and fired a mean stone missile at a great pace. We called them 'cataguns'. Not very original but we liked it.

The next part of this story involved me personally. I had done a swap with a school mate for his rather posh and very well made catapult gun for a rather boring jigsaw puzzle. I was very cocky with this catagun, making everybody jump when I was flashing it about. My mother would have had a 'duck fit' if she had known.

Like all good things, they come to an end and mine was a very abrupt one at that. It was a dark winter's evening and the street lamps – only gas in those days – were burning well. I was in one of my cocky catagun slinging moods swaggering up and down our street, brandishing my weapon to any kid who dared cross my path, like Ronald Reagan in one of those 'B' movies that were always showing at one of our many local cinemas in those days.

As the evening wore on and most of my mates had gone home, fed up with me peppering them with my catagun, I decided to look for new targets. This was my fatal move. The street lamps looked very inviting and a ready made target. So why not? I proceeded to take pot shots at the one adjacent to the local Off Licence. After a few direct hits I noticed that the remaining kids had left in rather a hurry and was left alone. Well not quite alone.

From across the road coming into the gloaming shed by the lamp was a very large dark figure, unmistakable as a policeman! Holy Cow!

The conversation was brief. The catagun was removed from my hand and the 'Bobby' laced into me with a verbal lashing of "How dare you?"

"Public property" etc. etc. – well, you can imagine, I was petrified. We were in those days. Fortunately the policeman had a good knowledge of the people on his patch and I didn't feature very high on his list of villains.

Alas the catagun went, never to return. I got a ticking off with the threat that he would tell my mother the next time I was found attempting to damage public property. A fate far worse than he could administer and he knew it. Subtle really. I suppose parents could punish us kids more effectively in those days as we had so little to start with, we treasured every possession we had and anything forfeited as a punishment really hurt. So we didn't do it. Well, not all of the time.

It was rare down our street to see a policeman who was not either walking or riding a bike. The idea of a police car driving around was usually restricted to the cinema and American gangsters. However, one day in late October, a few years after the war a police car was seen and heard, slowly crawling down our street with its loud hailer system booming out. Despite the crackles and whistling, we were all being warned that as November 5th was approaching and fireworks were on sale in the shops, we had to be on the look-out for some special and very dangerous ones.

Apparently an unauthorised batch of 'bangers' had been released to the shops with an extremely high content of gunpowder. A full description was called out from the police car and everyone was on their guard.

Well, nearly everyone. A very eccentric aunt of mine had unknowingly bought some of these 'bangers' for the usual family bonfire party to be held in her garden on top of the Anderson air-raid shelter which was still in position. These shelters, as well as offering us shelter from the German bombers (apart from a direct hit), were often used as storage inside and garden rockeries outside. My aunt's shelter was due for removal and this was to be the last time a bonfire was mounted on it. Now these bonfires could often be quite spectacular and be seen (and felt) by the neighbours in the next garden often to their great concern, as sparks would flood across their front door burning little pop marks in it and the surrounding paintwork which inevitably gave rise to sharp words, coupled with threats of the hosepipe being turned onto the bonfire if it wasn't controlled.

Alas, all of this paled into insignificance when the time came to light the fireworks. My aunt always insisted on lighting the fireworks and was to be seen mounting the Anderson shelter when the bonfire was suitably burned away allowing her to get as close as possible to it to get the maximum effect.

Little did she, or any of us for that matter, realise what was due to occur in those next few seconds. She always insisted on plenty of noise so the bangers were lit first. She only managed the first one. These dangerous 'bangers' which she hadn't bothered to check, were VERY dangerous! Crash, bang and wallop! The explosion could, I suspect, be heard some streets away plus the noise of shattering glass as the windows of the next door neighbour's house were blown in. Amazingly, my aunt's windows survived which did nothing to soothe the temper of her neighbour. They went crazy, calling the police who duly arrived in the same car with the loud hailer. It wasn't long before the reality of the situation was discovered and the offending 'bangers' were removed for safe keeping.

The feud with the neighbours continued for months. It wasn't until the husband of the house next door was struck down with a heart attack and my aunt, who was a trained war time nurse, saved him from choking on his tongue, that they all made up. Funny really that it takes some sort of emergency to get people together. The war proved that, with neighbours helping each other without question. But that old Anderson shelter had a lot to answer for on bonfire nights. It was eventually dismantled and carted off by the local council refuse department, leaving a large hole full of water. That was nothing new as it was full for most of the time. My Aunt was no fool; she converted it into a fish pond, much to the relief of the next door neighbours. They were sure that she wasn't so eccentric as to build a bonfire on water.

# CHAPTER 7

Down and around our street lived many odd characters and most of them just very ordinary folk with few complications. We did however have one family who were very well known throughout the country as the father was a boxing champion.

The young boys of this family were clearly intent from a very early age to follow in their father's footsteps and proceeded to pick fights with anybody and everybody. They were very big lads and no one could, even if they tried, get the better of them in a fight. They would swagger around the area provoking anybody that took their fancy and finishing up with a scrap which they always won, if it ever got started.

The local school teachers and shopkeepers were not free from their rather abrasive attitude and altercations were not uncommon with either category. It appeared that it was only their father who had any control over them, but as he was so often away at boxing venues, it was usually down to their mother, a meek soul, to sort out the messes into which they were prone to getting.

Alas, the two had few weaknesses to enable anyone to get their own back on these giant lads – and they were big – without running the risk of a bloody nose or a black eye. But as usual, enough pins can be stuck into an effigy to get some form of revenge and the day of reckoning did arrive and from a very unusual source.

These strapping lads did not suffer fools gladly and anyone who displayed any sign of weakness was immediately 'dealt with' – with one exception – and it was all to do with a misunderstanding. A group of the lads from our street were playing football in the playing field not far away, when the dreaded two were seen approaching. The lads toyed with the idea of clearing off to avoid any confrontation, but they decided to tough it out as they had taken with them a lad who had what we know today as cerebral palsy, called Martin and who had been looking forward to watching a bit of football in the open air, as he rarely got to the field.

The two 'toughs' inevitably seized the ball and started kicking it between themselves much to the annoyance of the gang. "Oy! Gives us the ball back you big bullies!" one brave soul shouted. That was it. The two chased the daring commentator across the field before running out of steam and returning to challenge anyone else who wanted a confrontation.

When suddenly and quite unexpectedly Martin bawled out in the clearest voice he could muster from his wheelchair "Give me my ball back!" You could have heard a pin drop. Nobody moved. What would the two toughs do now? Would they have a go at a crippled boy in a wheelchair? To everyone's amazement, one of the toughs picked up the ball and handed it to Martin, whose feeble and twisted hands held it tightly to his chest. The two just turned away without another word and strolled quietly away. No one breathed until they had disappeared from the field and out of earshot. Then there was the loudest cheer you ever heard! Martin was surrounded by the gang and was patted on the head and shoulders with wild enthusiasm. Nobody had dared face the dreaded pair before and it took a crippled lad who had achieved so little because of his disability, to defy the two.

News travelled fast. Martin was the hero of the hour. He was pushed up and down our street with all the other kids in the area being told of this miraculous event: "you'll never guess what Martin did today..."

It wasn't until Martin's mother heard about it that all became clear. Apparently, unbeknown to most of us kids , the two toughs from the boxing family had an elder brother who was confined to a mental home since he was a baby and lived entirely in wheelchair with no chance of release. The toughs used to visit him with their mother and she would relate to Martin's mother that the two younger boys were broken-hearted after these visits, as they could not bear to see their elder brother so disabled when they were so strong and healthy. Clearly Martin hit them in their weakest spot – their hearts. The toughs didn't appear again on the football field to menace the lads. But Martin was taken along each time – just in case!

We were blessed down our street with a few notable young girls of a forward nature. Good old Margie mentioned earlier, was really from the fourth division, in football parlance, but there were one or two more clearly heading for the first division. One such charmer was the most exotic red-headed girl you ever saw called Vivian, known to everyone as Viv. Thrusting young men would tear up the pavement to get at Viv. She had huge brown eyes that would melt one of Mr Polluci's ice-cream cornets at fifty paces.

Oh what joy it was when one of the more mature lads made a date with Viv. Not one of them could keep it to themselves and before long everybody knew where and when the lucky young buck was to entangle himself with the gorgeous one. This inevitably resulted in those not invited to participate in these grapplings (as that was what they always turned out to be) to follow at a discreet distance in the hope of a glimpse of bare flesh or some such stimulation. The last person you wanted on one of the jaunts was little Jimmy, whose exploits have been noted earlier in this missive. He could neither keep still or keep quiet as the episode in the woodshed amply demonstrated.

But it was to little Jimmy that the lads from our street were eternally grateful on one warm summer's evening. It had come to the attention of the 'head of espionage' down our street, one Harold Fidoe.

Clearly anybody with such a name came in for some stick. However, when after some years Harold shook off the inevitable aliases such as 'woofy', 'scratcher', 'patch' and 'shitty arse', he settled down to be commonly known as 'Barker'. He was a lad about sixteen and knew it all and usually he did.

Now, 'Barker' had picked up the scent (now you get the doggy connection) that one plucky youth called Adrian was to date the wonderful Viv, but no one had discerned the time or location of the liaison – except that was – yes, you've guessed it – little Jimmy who had intercepted a note from Viv which had been handed to his sister for onward transmission to the thrusting Adrian.

Oh what joy! The anticipation was almost too much for all those in the know to contain themselves! It was to be the parish hall after the Sunday school class had left that Adrian and Viv were to stay behind and hide at the back of the stage, normally the scene of 'An Inspector Calls' or a revival of 'Show Boat' and soon to be the venue of 'Lust in the Parish Hall' with a cast of two. The stage was normally curtained off from the main body of the hall, thus allowing anybody to lurk unseen when the Sunday School had finished. The idea was that 'Barker', a Sunday School teacher himself (he probably accounts for today's godless society on his own) would make sure that the rear door of the hall was left unlocked as he was the key holder that day. The chosen few were then to sneak in and get an eyeful of Viv and Adrian.

Whilst the rear door was open, nobody had checked the front door, which was soon to prove fatal.

Meanwhile Adrian and Viv had commenced 'proceedings' and the idea was that 'Barker' would pull back the curtains suddenly at a strategic moment revealing all (and it was all) to the waiting group.

Unknown to these budding voyeurs, the vicar and the church wardens were having a meeting in the upper room which doubled as a projection room for the weekly film evenings (pre-television days) and had come in by the front door and straight up the stairs to the room.

At the appointed moment, 'Barker' pulled back the curtain revealing the two, totally 'starkers', lying on a remnant settee from the last production.

The commotion drew the attention of the vicar and the church wardens to the observation window high up in the projection room. Well you can guess the rest – a major scrambling of bodies, both on and off the stage, and a rushing to the exits as fast as their legs would carry them. Rumour had it later when the news broke about the goings on, that Adrian – a mature youth – 'swished' off the stage holding and covering everything as he went. Whatever was showing seemed to impress the church warden, as Adrian was invited to tea shortly afterwards.

Oh, what I didn't relay earlier was that the church warden was a woman and an attractive widow at that. For a while, Adrian was off the Viv shopping list and pursuing activities of a more religious nature, or at least that was what he told us. Well, we were very young at the time!

Thinking of religion reminds me of the time the very same vicar who caught Adrian and Viv cavorting in the parish hall, went on a retreat leaving the two curates we had in those days, in charge for two weeks. These two, with help of a curate from an adjoining parish had longed for a period when they could express themselves as high churchmen and enjoy the ritual not normally practised at our church.

Apparently, one evening, when the vicar was 'retreating', these three set up an anointing ceremony normally reserved for the sick and dying, presumably imagining themselves as old testament worthies, blessing the Chosen Few. This included the using of the bishop's chair usually reserved for such visits from the hierarchy. A lot of incense was used during this ritual, to the point that the smoke alarm went off, resulting in the fire brigade coming and breaking down the front door of the church porch, only to find this quaint ceremony taking place. The vicar learned about this from the newspapers whilst on the retreat and immediately sped home to hold an investigation.

In true Church of England style, it was all hushed up only to blow up shortly afterwards when one of these curates was picked up by the police for committing a nuisance in a public toilet in the local park. They found his 'dog collar', in the back seat of his car covered by his cassock.

I suppose the oil anointing ceremony went to his head. Or something like that! There was a rumour – after he was asked to leave – that he went up to Scotland under the assumed name of 'Ben Doon'. I can't think why? But as I mentioned earlier, we were VERY young at the time.

# CHAPTER 8

Playing sport during those lengthy summer holidays was virtually our sole occupation as kids just after the war – when we had finished helping the milkman with his round. A few of the lads would congregate at the local recreation ground ready for cricket at the beginning of the holiday and switching to football at the end.

We had little by way of kit; usually just a bat and ball when it was cricket and no pads, despite the fact that we always used a hard ball made of compressed cork – we couldn't afford the real thing except when it was somebody's birthday. The wickets were chalked on the perimeter fence and off we went. This meant that shots behind the wicket were out, as too, was real fast bowling due to the lack of protection. The novelty of a cricket box came later, when there was something big enough to hit and protection duly followed.

This, however, did not rule out the odd ball finding a painful spot and the recipient howling and hopping about the place. Little sympathy was handed out and the game proceeded. One such incident involved a somewhat immobile lad called Bertie. He was regularly bruised and battered as his conception of keeping your eye on the ball was backing out of the way as fast as possible.

Poor Bertie not only had to contend with short pitched deliveries but also a very possessive mother. She would see the marks on Bertie's body on his return home at tea time and vow to knock the living daylights out of whoever was responsible for harming her treasured son. Despite Bertie's protests that it was all part of the game, she duly arrived at the door of one of the gang one day ready to carry out her threat. She had clearly got the wrong lad as the culprit, on the day in question, as she knocked on the door of a rather rough family who were not noted for their diplomacy down our street, nor for that matter their prowess at cricket. The door was answered by a large woman smoking a rather battered cigarette, which had been rolled rather badly and was hanging from the side of her mouth.

She leaned against the door jam, listening intently as Bertie's mother railed down her objections to her son being treated in this way and how his eye was now black and blue and so on. This went on for a minute or two with the cigarette ash getting longer and longer, when, without warning, this rough woman stepped back and delivered a right hook to the face of Bertie's mother. Down she clattered with legs and handbag flying into the bushes.

She scrambled up in a rather dishevelled manner, adjusting this and that and putting her cockeyed hat straight, but clearly backing away at least out of reach of another likely strike.

Bertie's mother, with a raised voice was, by now, well down the garden path, uttering confused threats to this woman, as she retreated, about the police having to be informed of this disgraceful behaviour and charges being brought. It cut no ice with this rotund and rather untidy woman. The cigarette by now was all ash. Bertie's mother knew it was time to return home in as dignified a manner as she could muster and did so, adjusting her hat, which was still at an angle, as she went.

It wasn't until a day or so later that the gang decided to call on Bertie to summon him to play cricket. The door was answered simultaneously by Bertie and his mother, both standing in the doorway with two of the biggest black eyes you ever saw. One each that is.

The gang could hardly contain themselves. With spluttering laughter, they inquired of Bertie's availability for cricket, but to no avail. They just collapsed with laughter and ran from the house telling everyone as they went and singing 'Two lovely black eyes – oh what a surprise' at the top of their voices.

Much to Bertie's mother's embarrassment, the local press got hold of the story. The headline in the evening paper was "TWO SHINERS FOR THE SHINERS". Yes, you've guessed it – their surname was Shiner. The whole story was laid out for all to see.

We didn't see much of Bertie at the recreation ground that summer. Can't think why? But we were very young at the time, you must remember.


One of the many thriving cinemas within walking distance was a small outfit known by the locals as 'The Flea Pit'. There are no prizes for guessing how this tag came about as it was a very small place holding no more than a hundred people at the most; all very close together.

The seats were uniquely priced, starting at six old pence and rising by three pence for every three or so rows, to the monumental heights of two shillings for a balcony seat. To call it a balcony was without doubt, an overstatement as it looked like a large wooden box pinned to the wall at the side.

From the seats priced at one shilling and sixpence and upwards, there were sprinkled around two-seaters to accommodate courting couples. Basically all they were two seats with the arm rests removed. Presumably, due to structural damage incurred by the more passionate amongst the clientele, the arms had previously been removed by them at strategic moments. The management, realising that they were on a loser, removed the arms as a matter of political discretion, not to mention the cost of replacing them every week with new ones.

These 'passion seats' as they were known, were in great demand with rows breaking out when more than one couple were trying to get them at the same time – and of course at the same price. Often couples were seen sneaking into a more expensive 'passion seat' when the manager wasn't looking. Often this led to them being caught out, with the humiliation of having to return from whence they came with heads bowed.

Needless to say, we kids were only too keen to get an eyeful of the steamy sessions going on in the 'passion seats', resulting in us missing most of the film on many an occasion.

What I could never understand was how these thrusting young lovers did not do themselves an injury with all that contortion going on and in full view of the rest of us too! Not to mention our cricked necks incurred by keeping an eye on the proceedings; but it was worth it, if only for educational purposes – well, I think that was what it was.

You could be watching Doris Day on the screen one minute, then an eyeful of thighs and suspender belts in the rear the next. All very confusing for a young boy, but we liked it really.

The inevitable crunch – so to speak – came when 'Pash Robbie', a well known occupant of these seats, with a wide variety of partners, was thrown out of 'The Flea Pit' when during one of his more heated sessions, he broke the 'passion seat' he was performing in. With a loud CRACK, the double seat crashed backwards into the row behind, resulting in the manager roaring down the aisle with his torch flashing (and that was not all that was flashing), proceeded to pull Robbie and his target for the night, into the street via the nearest exit.

That was how he got his nick name 'Pash' short for passion. He was quite a lad was 'Pash.' I reckon he had frequented virtually all the passion seats in 'The Flea Pit', but never with this result.

Unfortunately for 'Pash' he hadn't realised that he wasn't being thrown out solely for breaking the seat, but the female in question that evening was the manager's daughter! Whoops!


Despite having virtually every kind of shopping facility you care to mention down our street, there was no public convenience for anybody calling in on the area for a distance of over a mile.

For years, the council had planned to have one built but every time this cropped up, it was voted out by the planning committee for a variety of reasons, but basically because nobody wanted it built next to their shop or house. Spurious arguments raged for years as to whether we needed one at all, let alone where it should be built.

Things came to a head when the decision had to be made regarding the siting of a new bus shelter for the new bus company which was formed after the war. It seemed quite obvious that the 'new loo' – as it became known – should stand next to the shelter. All very simple you would think. Well, not quite.

It became a condition of the 'new loo' building that a survey had to be put in place to justify that one was needed in the first place. Back to square one.

Well now – who was going to undertake to do the survey? How would it be made up? The only way – the council decided – was to place next to the temporary bus stand – of course – a temporary loo! Then we could all see exactly what the demand was for this convenience. All very simple. Well... not quite again.

Those for the project set about to increase the numbers by enlisting a rosta of those of a like mind. They could be seen exercising their dogs, taking the kids out for a walk, almost everything was tried to make sure the temporary loo was used at all times. A counter was fixed to the door and off we went. Once the survey was over and all the figures were submitted to the Council and the usage fully justified, the Council Planning Committee decision day was fixed. All seemed to be set fair for a brand new bus shelter plus loo after all these years. Well... nearly.

One very well known opponent of the scheme was so incensed by all this jiggery pokery, he had, unknown to everyone, been keeping a log of all the people using the temporary loo, helped by one or two friends of like mind, and had drawn up a list of names of those who had used it repeatedly. The day before the council meeting, he had this list pinned to the council office noticeboard and contacted the local newspaper who took his photograph standing next to it with a placard saying "IT'S A FIX – WE'RE BEING PEED ON". The rest is history, as they say.

The council threw out the proposal by a big majority. The newspaper the next day had a banner headline – "PEE-PLE POWER WINS AGAIN". The loo was never built.

# CHAPTER 9

Entertainment was very much in the self-help category just after the war. This was coupled with the twice weekly trip to the cinema (pocket money permitting) and the obligatory Saturday night vigil at the Empire Theatre.

This wonderful Edwardian edifice was the pride of the folk, not just down our street, but of the whole town. It was built with marble outside and this was continued into the wonderful entrance with a sweeping two sided staircase to box office. The curving brass balustrade took your eyes up this beautiful entrance and into the ceilings which were covered in paintings of cherubs and semi-naked nymphs frolicking about with stringed instruments. They were always scantily clad in material which dangled tantalisingly across their vital parts. All very frustrating to a young lad like me just learning 'which does what with what'.

It was customary in our house that Mother took me to the Empire on Saturdays for the first house at about 6.30pm whilst Dad cleared off to the Club (a drinking den for members only). It was a real weekly treat so much so, that we had a permanent booking as did many other families, to avoid disappointment when popular shows were on.

I saw all the great music hall personalities and especially those from the radio whose voices we knew, but had never seen in the flesh. During the summer months it switched to a repertory company with weekly plays and a resident company. This gave the resident orchestra a break from their twice nightly performances, much to the delight of the Leader; a man called Bill. Now Bill was prone to a tipple or two before during and after the performances. His antics were well known by the whole town but it only added spice to the proceedings as nobody (including Bill) knew what was likely to occur as the evening progressed.

During the warm evenings before the orchestra (something of an over-rated description, if I remember) went off on holiday and the actors moved in, the roof of the theatre could be opened by some sort of sliding mechanism to allow the place to ventilate. Nobody had heard of air conditioning in those days. It was a great spectacle to see the cherubs and nymphs sliding into each other's private parts, revealing the sky to the aghast audience, which usually responded with a round of applause. That was until an odd and unexpected rain cloud would hasten the closing of the roof with a shower onto the stalls below. This had the effect of a short but poignant round of heckling from those quietly being drenched.

But quite the most spectacular event happened during the performance of a touring opera group who were singing popular arias. We had balcony seats with an uninterrupted view of the stage and the orchestra. On these occasions Bill the leader would normally have to step down to allow the singers own conductor to take over the performance, but on this particular night, Bill was called upon to take over the baton, with disastrous results.

He had had more than a few drinks before the show and was seen in the bar during the interval knocking the whiskies back with some regularity.

Quite out of the blue and not connected with Bill, someone no more than a few rows in front of us in the balcony stood up during this second half aria and threw up over all the rows in the balcony below himself and into the lower stalls. There was pandemonium. People screaming and shouting and calling for the manager.

Meanwhile Bill carried on regardless with the aria, which was being sung by a very busty lady. Eventually he could stand the noise of people jumping up and down no longer. He turned round very quickly too – quickly as it turned out – lost his balance due, we all thought, to the last few drinks during the interval and crashed headlong into the violins just to his left.

Further pandemonium broke out. What with people trying to get cleaned up from the phantom 'thrower upper' and Bill and violins rolling around in the orchestra pit, the scene was without doubt the high spot of the show. The singer, to her eternal credit, carried on regardless.

No, she wasn't singing 'Nessun Dorma', but there was certainly nobody sleeping in the Empire Theatre that night.


Far removed from the Empire Theatre environment, but not in distance, was the beach; not a pretty beach by any standards with the steelworks and engineering factories right next to it, but it was a haven of refuge for all the folk in the area around our street as they enjoyed walks along the promenade and an ice-cream on a Sunday afternoon.

A walk along the beach was well nigh impossible due to the raw sewage that was washed back from the outflow pipe some hundred yards out to sea. However, the seaside was free and we made the most of it.

It is hard to imagine that not only did the beach entertain hazards from the sewage outflow, but it was the centre of a thriving industry which came ashore quite naturally called sea coal. This area was not far from the coal mines just along the coast, many of which went out for miles under the sea. Some of the seams of coal were very near the surface and, with the movement of the tide, would skim the surface of the sea bed and release the coal which was washed onto the beach. It was open house for anybody to rake up this sea coal and either use it themselves or sell it to the people of the area, as it was very good quality, being very fine and easily burnt. But as the price of real coal rose, the clamour for sea coal became more intense. So much so that when the tide was coming in and just on the turn, the sea coal gatherers would be there in their dozens with rakes at the ready. The jostling for a good pitch was one thing but the means of transport to cart it away was another.

They came in all shapes and sizes – horse drawn carts, hand carts, bicycles, prams and for the really serious – huge ex-army lorries with high chassis which were able to get into the water ahead of the rest. The competition was fierce, resulting in devious moves by the 'big boys' with the trucks, keeping out the little guys, by making barriers across the beach with their trucks, thus protecting the best collection areas.

Needless to say, this got into the local press with headlines such as "SEA COAL MAFIA BOSSES CONTROL BEACH". All very exciting to us kids. We would scuttle down to the sea coal areas to witness any 'shoot outs' just like James Cagney, but usually all we saw was boring old sea coal being raked in by boring old grown ups.

It wasn't long before these territorial disputes came to a head revolving around one particular and very large – both in size and wallet – bloke called 'Hossy'. He came by the name as he used to do most of his business with a horse and cart before the war, but had graduated to several ex-army trucks to do his sea coal business. 'Hossy' must have weighed about twenty stones and always wore a filthy suit and a trilby hat, which was all greasy and bashed in. It was his trucks that were blockading the beach and his name stank with all the other gatherers. They decided enough was enough, and somehow 'Hossy' had to have his 'wings clipped'. But how?

A 'council of war' was drawn together by the other gatherers in the back room of the Seven Stars pub not far from the beach. Everyone made sure that 'Hossy' was kept well away from the meeting. One 'hen-pecked' gatherer's wife was a particular target for the over indulgent 'Hossy' and she was given the unenviable task of getting 'Hossy' drunk at the British Legion Club in the town centre. He thought he was about to get the fruits of his desires with this rather brassy wench, but was really having his future mapped out for him just down the road.

After about an hour or two's drinking, 'Hossy' was well and truly pickled. Meanwhile, the secret meeting had completed its deliberations and a plan was afoot.

During the next few days, the tide was turning in the late afternoon and, as it was winter, it was getting dark at about 4 pm. The brassy wife was again called upon to make the supreme sacrifice and tempt 'Hossy', down to the Legion again for a heavy lunchtime session prior to him going down to the beach for the big rake up. He was sporting only one lorry that day and he was the driver.

Meanwhile, down at the beach, the other gatherers were literally laying in a trap for big 'Hossy'. They had dug a huge trench across the entrance to the beach, just far enough along to enable 'Hossy' to get onto the sand and then – BINGO! – down he would go, truck and all. They all parked their motley array of carts and bikes at the other side of the trench which was covered with cardboard with sand on top showing nothing of their potential scene of triumph in just a few short minutes.

Meanwhile, back at the Legion , the brassy wife was really brassed off by this time. Big 'Hossy' had been trying all sorts of tricks to get her into his truck which was parked outside, but to no avail. She eventually persuaded him that "time and tide literally wait for no man" and proceeded to get 'Hossy' to the door and into his lorry. Down at the beach all the others were waiting, some with a genuine fear of what 'Hossy' might do when all was revealed and he was six feet below sea level. They didn't have to wait long. The rumbling of that familiar ex-army truck could heard a mile away. The tide meanwhile was coming in dead on time and the light was dimming fast. The rumbling of the truck was getting nearer and all at the other side of the trap were getting very jumpy indeed. The truck at last came into view and proceeded onto the sand. It was within a few yards of the trap when all of a sudden it stopped short. A air of sheer panic spread amongst the gatherers. What was he playing at? The lorry engine was turned over but nothing happened.

"Oh my God" said one of the ring leaders, " he's broken down!" The engine turned again success – it started, but it didn't move. The engine whined and wheels went round, but the lorry remained stationary. It was well and truly stuck in the sand.

After what seemed an age, the door of the truck opened and a figure got out, not from the driver's side, but the passenger door. In the gloom which by now was enveloping the beach, a small figure clambered down from the lorry and walked towards the waiting crowd on the other side of the trap and shouting: "Give us a push will yer?" The voice was familiar and the figure known to many a man in the area. It was the brassy wife! She clearly hadn't shaken off the dreaded 'Hossy' and was waddling towards the trap in her high heels, being well-sloshed from her afternoon at the Legion trying to drink 'Hossy' under the table.

"STOP! STOP! STOP! " came the shout of her husband from along the beach, but it was too late. With legs akimbo and handbag aloft, she clattered through the cardboard cover and into the trap, with a God-Almighty scream! The watching crowd ran forward with torches as by now it was almost dark. There she lay, displaying all the parts that 'Hossy' had spent all afternoon trying to reach.

She was hauled out, none the worse for wear and carried off the beach by a few willing hands. Meanwhile everybody had forgotten big 'Hossy', still in the truck. They gingerly walked over and looked in. There he was, fast asleep and snoring his head off, pissed as a fart.

He had, it seems, seen nothing and was content to wait for help immediately falling asleep at the wheel.

Well, the story ends there, but rather than waste the plan altogether, the other gatherers filled in the trap and sent for the police. 'Hossy' was done for being found drunk in charge of a vehicle which was uninsured and not taxed for which he was fined and suspended from driving for three months. He still knew nothing of the great beach trap years later, as nobody had the guts to tell him, for fear of reprisals.

As for the brassy wife, she was eventually caught by big 'Hossy' and went to live with him after something of a scandal.

The only comment I heard about the affair was from my mother, who was heard to reflect on this new relationship:

"I'd rather sleep with a bag of sea coal than 'im". I couldn't see the point myself – but I was young at the time.

# CHAPTER 10

One part of our street which got little attention was the Free Church chapel, which was situated virtually on its own with a garden surrounding it.

They tended to keep themselves to themselves at the chapel, as most of the people down and around our street attended the Church of England church that has been mentioned earlier in this missive. But once a year, the chapel came into everybody's focus when it was eisteddfod time.

Now why it was called Eisteddfod, when we were hundreds of miles from Wales, always puzzled me. I suppose today we would call it an Arts Festival as it had music and verse of all types.

I always got dragged along by my neighbour who was keen on that sort of thing, but frankly, I would rather have been on the recreation ground with the lads. But I always remember certain highlights that have stuck in my mind from those days and which still tickle the old chuckle-bone.

One particular one was when an old lady, very much past her best as a singer, always insisted in giving a rendering of "Where the bee sucks there suck I". These words always made us all laugh as they were very easily distorted to a naughty version, rather like the village of Uckington, where the name of the village was constantly being added to by the local youths. However, that aside, this poor old dear on what was to be her last appearance, came to the end of her song; turned round to leave the stage after her bow, only to reveal that she had her dress tucked into her knickers. The audience collapsed with laughter.

I don't think she ever knew why the normally serious song was a matter of such hilarity.

Or the time old Joe the Sextant was reciting a poem which had the words "thou my dear will form my art" which stumbled out as "thou my dear will arm my fart". Nobody laughed but there was a lot of sniggering in the back row.

The pastor at the chapel usually compered the show and the mayor presented the prizes. Alas, the pastor had the most awful drawl of a stammer, which added at least ten minutes to the already boring proceedings.

All the sections were competitive and the judging was a very serious affair, with panels for each category sitting at the side, making copious notes, which probably in truth was the weekend shopping list, or the week's selections for the football pools which had just started. During one of the singing competitions for "Ladies of Mature Years", one old dear, realising that things weren't going so well, started a little dance during the reprise, which included the lifting up of her dress revealing, at the audience level, (something she had overlooked) a pair of bright red bloomers. This did the pastor no good at all.

His next item of introduction took at least an extra five minutes for him to spit out a choral number based on the hymn: "As pants the heart for cooling streams".

Then there was that disastrous time a visiting choir was using an old school form for the back row to stand on, when one of them lost his balance, pulling the rest down and backwards into the rear curtain. Unfortunately, this rear area was doubling as the ladies changing room and the weight of the falling bodies pulled down the curtain altogether, revealing an assortment of semi-clad females diving for cover. My view with hindsight is that they should have charged more for the entrance fee, as on occasions, it rivalled the slapstick cinema of Laurel and Hardy.

As well as being dragged along to the Eisteddfod, we kids were expected to toddle along with parents to the various garden parties given in aid of some charity or other. These do's took the form of a tea and bun fight alongside a raffle and a game of progressive whist; all in somebody's house that had a decent sized garden, large enough to get about twenty or so people in it.

The average age of those attending looked to about ninety to us kids, with most of them sporting some form of blue dye to their hair or a heavy wash in peroxide. It was very civilised and extremely boring for us, but the expectation of a good tea with cakes, jelly and ice-cream, was a big inducement.

Whilst the grown-ups got stuck into the whist drive, we kids had to entertain ourselves without leaving the house. We contrived all sorts of games for hours on end until we ran out of ideas, until one day, Maurice, a somewhat studious boy, who was known as Mozzy, decided that even he was cheesed-off with the situation and set to do something about it.

Mozzy was known as a collector of queer things which he would often bring to show us. He didn't collect the usual boys' items such as cigarette cards or stamps; oh no; he had boxes full of dead spiders and cards with flies skewered to them in neat little rows. We always thought he was a 'screw ball', but anything out of the ordinary to relieve the monotony was welcome.

Often we kids were given the task of decorating the garden with streamers and we had to make our own from whatever bits of tissue paper we could find. This was where the "Mozzy collections" came in handy. He would turn up with all sorts, then get us all to sort them out and string them up from trees and bushes in the garden. On one such occasion, he amazingly produced half a dozen balloons, which were like gold dust at the time of rationing. We were all very impressed and proceeded to inflate them and string them up in the trees just before this particular garden party got underway.

It was rather a warm day and the temperature was rising very quickly with everyone reaching for their straw hats and any shady parts of the garden they could find. The place looked very nice and the parents congratulated us kids for our efforts and decided to give us an early tea which pleased us no end.

It got hotter and hotter with everyone discreetly wiping the sweat from their necks, when there was an almighty BANG! The whole place shuddered to a stand still. BANG! again, and BANG! again! The balloons were exploding with the heat.

It wasn't until Mozzy's father appeared to join in the party that things went rapidly 'downhill'. You see, Mozzy with his insatiable appetite for collecting things, had stumbled across a packet of 'French Letters' in his father's bedside drawer and had assumed in his ignorance that they were balloons.

As his father surveyed the scene the 'balloons' went off one by one – six in all, leaving those tell-tale rubber sleeves with little knobs on the end, dangling from the trees.

Of course we innocents weren't supposed to know what they were, but we were well ahead of the rest when it came to 'French Letters' and proceeded to snigger as Mozzy's dad quickly started pulling these 'balloons' from the trees when it became clear who had provided them. There was a stony silence as the offending items were taken down and Mozzy's mum and dad beat a hasty retreat with Mozzy in tow.

Now this was embarrassing enough, but the fact that Mozzy's family were staunch Roman Catholics was what caused the mutterings from the rest of gathered throng. Needless to say, Mozzy's family were conspicuous by their absence for some while until the story died down.

The sequel to the story was that Mozzy's mother gave birth to a set of twins less than a year later and the whole family were to be seen at the Confessional each Sunday, presumably seeking divine intervention, as the plain brown parcels stopped coming through the post, with this unexpected result – especially as Mozzy's dad was the local postman!


One of the regulars of the gang down our street was a lad we nicknamed Alipan. He was called Alan really but he seemed to spend most of his time eating in the kitchen – that's where the pan bit came in.

He had another name which was used when we could stand his eating habits no longer – 'Tweet', as he was always saying "I'm just going in for something to eat" – which nearly sounded like Tweet. Anyway, that is how I remember him. He was a latter day Billy Bunter and looked like him too.

He, needless to say, was the school goalkeeper in winter and the wicket keeper in summer as he was so large, not letting anything past him no matter what size ball.

When threatened by anybody foolish enough to try, he would merely thrust his stomach at them and that usually did the trick. He had a genial face, all round and red, which complemented his frame very nicely. I suppose he weighed in at about ten stones when only about twelve years of age: he was quite a boy.

He also had an amazing soprano voice which was clear as a bell, which resulted in him being him in great demand in the local choirs as a boy soloist. But all he wanted to do apart from sport was to ring the church bells. This was arranged as a trial by the local tower captain and with some trepidation, a date was fixed for Alipan to have a go. Apart from his obvious weight, he was immensely strong for his age and within no more than a few peals he had cracked the wooden bell supports and stopped the peal. It was suggested that he stick to singing instead, to prevent any more damage.

The church choir stalls for the boys were simply not big enough for Alipan, so he had to sit with the men on the back row which made him feel important as well as being able to sit down in comfort. In the days before the organ bellows were automated and hand filling was done by revolving a large wheel, Alipan over-pressurised the system by pumping too fast with the result that the bellows split and the organ sagged to a standstill. Alipan simply couldn't get it right.

One lasting memory of him was when, during a football match, with him in goal as usual, he dived at a shot near the post; crashed into it, and it bent and simply stayed there as it was made of steel tubing. All efforts to straighten the post failed, so the match was moved to another pitch nearby.

As he grew older, Alipan got larger. To everyone's amazement, some years later he announced that he was getting married to a lovely girl called Anna. She was almost as big as Alipan and when the wedding day came, the aisle of the church was too narrow to get them both down side by side, so they left by the side door!

You can only guess at their sleeping arrangements.

# CHAPTER 11

The arrival of the evening newspaper was always a feature in most of the homes down our street. Almost to a man (or woman) the first page turned to was the births, marriages and deaths, better known as the hatched, matched and despatched page.

These columns kept everyone up to date with families at the other side of the town, despite the fact that they lived no more than half an hour's walk away. We were very parochial in those days. The advent of the motor car some years later put paid to all that.

It always seemed to me that the deaths column had a weird fascination for my parents with Father leading off.

"Well I never – Geordie Smales has died."

"He never 'as!"

"Aye – the poor old bugger."

"He was no age." ("He must have been SOME age you daft old bat!")

"Aye – only 55."

"What was wrong?"

"I heard he had the big 'C' – liver yer know."

"That's what comes of boozin' down the club every night – you'll be next."

"Sod off."

"All our family died clean deaths" – mother would always insist that most of her family died of anything but the big 'C'. As the result was the same, I could never see the point of the argument.

The attendance at funerals by grown-ups was mandatory. It was often the only time they saw their friends altogether in one place. The conversations were always the same at the tea party afterwards.

"Ee – I only saw him last week. He looked fine then."

"I know – it must have come on quite sudden like."

"Aye – but did you see him at the funeral home? He didn't look too good then."

"Well, he wouldn't yer daft bugger, would 'ee?" said with a discrete cackle.

"They say he couldn't keep his food down for the past few weeks."

"You could have bloody well fooled me – he was knockin em back at the club last week, I was told by his sister – you know, the one with the long nose that goes to shoppin' in those ridiculous high heels. She 'ad no time for 'im, I was told."

"Aye, but I see she's turned up today – she'll be after that tea service in the china cabinet – you know, the one with gold edging."

"Poor old bugger – he'll be turning in his grave already."

Yes, these funerals certainly had the feeling of goodwill and family harmony stamped right through them.

Now, if funerals had their charms then baptisms, or christenings, as we used to say, had something else: usually a whole lot of noise and mayhem. But nothing compares with the incident at the baptism font when I was a choir boy. We took turns in attending the vicar as a server, handing out service sheets and generally feeling important. On one particular day, we had a special baptism for one baby boy of about eighteen months old. He had been in hospital for a long period after his birth and had not been baptised. The snag was that this boy was by now well and truly a bouncing baby, so much so, that the vicar had visited the house for a practice hold ready for the Sunday afternoon service.

When the moment came for the vicar to administer the water, the baby boy was so violent that the vicar slowly lost his grip and the baby slipped gently into the font head first. After a hasty intervention by the verger all was well, and the baby was taken home wet through, with the baptism completed in double quick time and mumblings from the parents: "'Ee wants lockin' up that vicar – too bleedin' old if you ask me!"

But without doubt, weddings featured highly on the list of church entertainment in those days before the video recorders. Alas, everything is committed to memory – but what memories!

It was the ritual that the cross was carried ahead of the bride when she entered the church.   On one occasion, on a late Saturday afternoon, the male server had attended the previous wedding held in the morning and had been invited to the reception.   Known for his ability at glass lifting as well as cross-carrying, the person in question, called Dave, turned up at the afternoon wedding well and truly drunk.

He had kept well away from the vicar prior to the service and had made his way gingerly to the front door of the church, fully robed and carrying the cross.

The bride duly arrived, the music had begun, and Dave started the procession up the aisle followed by the vicar, bride and proud father and the toddling bridesmaids.

Following a distinctly wavering path, Dave made it to the chancel steps, only to run out of steam and slowly, but very slowly, he sank to his knees and the cross was 'parked' in the large display of flowers at the side of the chancel steps.   The verger again came to the rescue and removed Dave and the cross, to their respective places.   Dave wasn't asked again to display his talents at cross-bearing and went off to be an pilot in the RAF with surprisingly few accidents to his name.

One of the more unsung services of the church (no pun intended) was confirmation.   Probably the most vivid part was that all the girls wore rather silly white table clothes over their heads, whilst the boys wore nothing.   On their heads I mean. Some old bishop would turn out to lay his hands on the candidates making them full members of the church.   But, as far as I was concerned, it meant that you could take communion and that meant a swig of wine each time you went.   This was great stuff for us young kids, so confirmation couldn't come quickly enough.

The only snag was that the old bishop was well past his sell-by date and proceeded to address the congregation:

"Dearly beloved, we are gathered here to join together this man and this woman in Holy Matrimony". The chaplain quickly interjected with the correct version, otherwise it could have turned out as one of the biggest weddings in the church's history!

Now this "Laying On Of Hands", as it used to be called, had its problems, and it wasn't until a rather bizarre incident occurred that I understood why the girls wore these white cloths on their heads. It was customary for the boys and girls to kneel before the bishop; he would place his hand on each person and say the necessary prayer. This was fine until a boy called Billy came forward with a corresponding girl partner. After the prayer, the girl rose and returned to her seat, but Billy went nowhere. He had an abundance of curly hair and the Bishop's ring had apparently become caught in it, resulting in Billy yelling and firmly rooted in the kneeling position. Yet again the valiant Verger came to the rescue, unhitching Billy and the Bishop.

Now I realised why the girls wore the head dress. But the Bishop's earlier gaff about 'joining everybody together' seemed appropriate now.

Scandal in church ranks always had more spice to it than normal and ours was no exception. The bringing of girls into the choir was bound to tempt Providence and it did.

One very 'forward' girl who had joined, despite protestations from virtually everybody, very soon became embroiled with one of the younger men who sat on the back row and whose voice had changed, but everything else was very active!

It took no more than six months and it happened. The choir parents were summoned to the vicarage to be told that the young lady in question was 'up the spout' and would be getting married in two weeks' time, stressing to the other parents the dangers of sexual promiscuity outside marriage.

Amazingly, the wedding was held in church with the full choir and all the trappings. It wasn't until the first hymn was announced that decorum and straight faces broke down. The vicar, without a flicker, said:

"The first hymn will be 'Dear Lord and Father of mankind, forgive our foolish ways, reclothe us in our rightful minds, in purer lives thy service find'." Not one face was to be seen, as hymn books were held across faces and a good deal of shaking was evident.


The induction of the new vicar was a somewhat hilarious event too. Invitations had gone out to all neighbouring vicars and their flocks asking how many seats they required as the church could only hold so many. This included the dean from our cathedral. What the dean did not know, was that someone had sent a second list in.

On the day of the induction, all the processions came into the church with the bishop waiting for everyone to take their places whilst a hymn was being sung, in came the dean and his procession of about half a dozen bods, lead by the cathedral cross-bearer. Coming to the appointed seats, to their surprise they found them already occupied by the party with duplicate tickets. The dean and his party were by now holding up the whole affair, so the cross bearer was instructed to do another circuit of the church, assuming a miracle would happen, as all the obvious seats were jam-packed full.

Dutifully, the dean's procession circled the church, only to return to the appointed spot, which was still fully occupied. There being no obvious solution, the cross-bearer was urged to make yet another circuit. By now the bishop and his party –

still waiting for the dean and his lot to park up – were virtually in hysterics.

Eventually, with a fourth circuit looming, the dean instructed the cross-bearer and the rest to stand at the back of the church until emergency chairs could be found.

The bishop's chaplain was overheard to say: "The church is always going round in circles – so what's new?"

At the inquest later, it was discovered that the party occupying the dean's seats was organised by a woman who had a crush on the dean and was regularly being told to politely get stuffed. On realising she had the dean's seats, she removed the sign on it and threw it on the floor.

Well, as the old saying goes: 'Hell hath no fury like a woman with a mission', or something like that.

# CHAPTER 12

Progress wasn't a word often heard around our street as most people were set about the daily task of simply surviving from one pay day to the next. That was those that had jobs, which oddly enough was most people in those days after the war.

But progress did arrive at the doorstep of the most unlikely person in the shape of our milkman. Having struggled with a push cart for most of his life and graduating to horse and cart, which eventually died, the idea of a motor truck was unthinkable. Nevertheless, the milkman, quite out of the blue, came into a small legacy from an aged aunt who had recently slipped off her mortal coil and left him £500, 'to do with as he pleased' as the Will stated.

A small pick-up style truck was duly purchased second hand from a scrap metal merchant and arrived with the beaming milkman at the wheel and quickly pressed into service. The efficiency of the milk round shot up, being completed in half the time, which meant that the milkman himself was finished his round by about 11am. Immediately, thoughts of expansion came readily to the milkman. Incidentally, his name was Rodney, often shortened to Rod but extended again by those who new of his exploits to 'Hot Rod'; no prizes for guessing the origin of the 'Hot' bit. His more attentive lady customers were only too aware of his prowess and the idea that he may have more time on his hands to pay due regard to their needs and wants, was very exciting indeed. But Rod had other ideas. He planned to create a major expansion of his round and yet still be home by lunchtime. Well, that WAS the plan. Alas, poor old Rod was often the victim of circumstance and there was another cock-up lurking just around the corner, like the time somebody tried to con him into taking up a job with a vast salary, as a pork pie salesman in Golders Green. He noticed at the last moment that the job was offered on April 1st!

Leaflets were duly printed and circulated to all the customers of his rivals in the area: "Get your milk in double quick time from our new motorised delivery service." The orders came flooding in and his target was reached with no effort. Every day, nearly twice the number of customers got their milk from Rod and he was still home for lunch and all because of his truck.

All this activity left Rod quite exhausted, despite being home for lunch. His more ardent female customers were being deprived of their usual slap and tickle and were becoming restless. All Rod wanted after the daily round was a long snooze with his feet up. However, his female admirers had not long to wait for their luck to return. The new part of his expanded milk-round was up a very steep hill which normally was out of the question with the old hand cart. The truck would roar up the hill in no time and slide back down with no effort whatsoever. Unfortunately for Rod, the scrap merchant from whom he had bought the truck had failed to draw one or two defects to his attention, with catastrophic results one Saturday morning.

Trying to finish even earlier to get to the football match, he was seen to be roaring around as usual and had just completed the new customers up the hill, when, on his return downhill, he noticed that he was steadily being overtaken by a wheel. The wheel was at first glance very familiar – neatly painted white walls – oh no! At that point the truck had a mind of its own, turning slowly right, when clearly Rod wanted it to go left. Suddenly, the front of the truck came up towards Rod and a gigantic crashing sound came from the rear. The truck then spun at speed and into the gable end of the British Legion Club. The whole of a very low window fell majestically into the road revealing several shocked early drinkers (it was barely midday), who simply moved with their drinks to the far side of the room as if in some slow motion film.

That was the end of Rod's ambitions. The truck was wrecked and within two days, all the customers he had pinched from his rivals went crawling back, as his hand cart wasn't up to it. Nor was he, for that matter, although he always seemed to have time to attend to his female admirers; truck or no truck.

Now, no street would be complete without its own window cleaner and our street was no exception. Ours rejoiced in the name of Clarence, but was better known to his friends as Clarry.

Now Clarry was without doubt the eyes, ears and on some occasions the nose of the whole area around our street. In short, he was the biggest gossip of all time, which included all the females in the butcher's queue on a Saturday morning, bar none.

The trouble with Clarry was that he simply could not keep out of other peoples' business and, having done so, then go on to 'spill the beans' to everybody in the neighbourhood about what he had learned. This was usually the format, but, on occasions, he had his uses in other directions. If anybody wanted to put about a rumour, all you had to do was engage Clarry in light unassuming conversation such as:

"Hey Clarry, have you, er, heard about number forty-two's goings on?"

"No, no I haven't – what's going like? Your secret's safe with me pet. I'm the soul of discretion."

At this point, all you had to do was to put down a few hints that all was not well at number forty two between 'im an' 'er and you know who,' and before you said 'knife' it was down and around the street in a flash. How he survived the war was beyond comprehension, as it was everybody's duty to not pass on rumours! For the record, Clarry was seconded to a reserve occupation during the war and was sent to a well-known glass factory in the north-west, which is where we assume, he got the bug for window cleaning when it was all over.

One area where Clarry really came into his own was passing on veiled threats made by the local Bobby, especially to wayward kids who were causing a problem and were due for the 'high jump' if they didn't watch out.

One such youth was a kid called Freddie, known locally as 'Freddie the Fox', because he was a cunning little twerp and constantly in trouble with the police and our local bobby in particular.

On one such occasion, Freddie was leading gangs of kids, usually younger than himself, into breaking into derelict property and stripping out the lead pipes and flogging it to the local scrap yard. He then shared out the money – well not exactly shared equally. The younger kids got a few pence while Freddie got the bulk of the haul all to himself. The trouble was that the police simply couldn't catch Freddie at it and nobody would 'snitch' on him as he had a nasty streak which often resulted in the odd black eye.

Getting fed up with this lack of results, the local bobby decided to engage the considerable talent of good old window cleaner Clarry. A plot had to be hatched and Clarry was to be the 'agent provocateur', which pleased him no end, as he had a vivid imagination most of the time.

It was an ambitious plan but it was guaranteed to catch Freddie red-handed with no means of escape, as in the past the Bobby had Freddie in view but couldn't catch him in the resulting chase.

The scene of this melodrama was to be the nearby sack making factory. Jute sacks were made from materials shipped in from India and sewn together by a load of females who worked at their stitching machines and sang at the top of their voices all the latest songs accompanied by relay radio, a form of cable radio, transmitted from a shop in the main high street. This technology was far removed from the transistor radio which was some years away from being invented. It was not a good idea for any strange man, or any man for that matter, to stray into the factory area unaccompanied. These rather rough

girls were no strangers to a bit of sexual harassment and it was
not unknown for them to grab an unsuspecting male, strip him
and throw him into the street, or even worse, stick his private
parts into a milk bottle and then start to excite him, with very
painful results!  However, all this aside, the manager of the
factory was tipped off about the plot to secure a charge against
Freddie, which pleased him no end, as Freddie had done him
over in the past and got away with it.  The roof of the factory
was edged with lead flashings recently replaced since Freddie's
last 'visit' and all was set for big moment.  Clarry had been
tipped off that he should tip Freddie the wink that there was to
be no working at the factory on Saturday, as it was their annual
works outing to Whitby that day and the place was shut and
totally empty.  Freddie could hardly contain himself.  The idea
of another big haul with nobody around was too good to miss.

Satisfied that Freddie had taken the bait, the local Bobby
stationed himself in the manager's office which overlooked the
factory floor and also had a view of the perimeter fence.  As
the evening turned to dusk, Freddie made his move.  With his
wheelbarrow positioned alongside the factory wall for a quick
getaway, Freddie climbed the fence and dropped into the yard
of the factory.  He quickly made his way to the side wall of the
factory which still had a vertical ladder attached to it, a remnant
of wartime fire watching, and up he went, catlike and very
quietly.  The bobby could see all and stealthily made his way to
a roof hatch adjacent to the manager's office.  He was
determined to catch him in the act and this he thought, was the
only way.

Meanwhile, Freddie was stripping away at the lead and
throwing it onto bales of completed sacks awaiting shipment at
the base of the factory wall.  The bobby made his move:

"Halt, in the name of the Law!" – it was very formal in
those days – shouted the bobby.  Freddie, almost jumping out
of his skin, realised that he was almost within arm's length of
the officer.  The bobby in his excitement, went to grab Freddie
but lost his footing on the sloping roof.  He fell backwards onto

the slated roof and skidded majestically downwards and off the edge!

The bales of sacks broke his fall, but as he was quite a big fellow, he bounced from one bale to another, but did not quite make it and slid between the two and was firmly stuck. Freddie, realising his luck, took the same route as the bobby had, but with perfect execution and hopped over the fence and away.

It wasn't until a passing drunk coming home from the pub at about midnight, heard the shouts of the bobby coming from his rather squashed position between the bales, that the alarm was raised. Alas the drunk, having raised the alarm, failed to make himself scarce, with the result that the bobby, duly released, found him fast asleep against the factory wall and 'nicked' him for being drunk and incapable. I suppose he was so miffed at losing Freddie, he had to take it out on somebody.

Freddie was eventually caught attacking the church roof and being cornered by the vicar's Alsatian dog, gave himself up. He asked at the court for all the other offences to taken into consideration, including the sack factory. But he insisted on blurting out to the magistrate about the bobby and the roof fall. The local newspaper was headlined the next day 'Policeman Fails To Get His Man – But Got The Sack Instead'. As usual, Freddie had the last laugh and six months inside.

Clarry, meanwhile unrewarded for his efforts to corner Freddie, was back to his usual occupation as a full time gossip and a part-time window-cleaner. Putting aside his talent as a police informer, he resorted to his normal stance of looking into his clients' houses from his perch on his ladder. As with all good things, they eventually come to an end and Clarry poked his nose in once too often.

Part of his round took him to the house of that floozy who used to cavort in front of the window of her bedroom a couple of doors down from our house. She eventually started to put her more unusual talent to practical use, when she got tangled up with several married men in the area. These guys could be seen at night beckoning her from the garden to come down from her bedroom and er 'play', I suppose. Well, we were very young at the time. One even used to shine his torch on his private parts to tempt her down. I knew this, as I overheard my mother telling her neighbour:

"That dirty bugger from Chapel View Lane was round last night flashing his torch at the floozy again – and that's not all he was flashing!"

"Never," said our neighbour Daisy.

"Oh aye – you could see it as plain as a pike staff – well not quite as big as a pike staff – if you know what I mean Daisy," said mother, rather getting out of her depth.

"They reckon they call him Big Dick Hampton down at the Club," retorted Daisy somewhat excitedly.

"Can't think why" said mother rather naively.

Realising she was getting somewhat flustered, mother changed the subject and headed for the butcher's – where else?

Clarry, meanwhile, was continuing his surveillance of the floozy, who got wind that he was the carrier of the tales of her exploits and confronted him with it.

Whilst this would normally be the thing to do in such circumstances and at street level, she waited until he was at her bedroom window. With one push, she heaved Clarry backwards off the ladder and into the rose bushes below. Scratched and torn, Clarry sheepishly made an exit homewards with tales of how a dog startled him, resulting in the fall. Poor old Clarry! He never could keep his mouth shut.

# CHAPTER 13

Adjacent to the timber yard just off our street was the yard belonging to the local coal merchant called Roger.

We kids would hang around Roger's yard, waiting for the cart to leave and hop on it when the first bag of coal was delivered. As we couldn't physically lift the bags of coal, that's all we could do apart from feed the horse and clean out the stable. Yes, this was a one-horse power cart and was totally reliable at that.

The yard was next to the railway sidings, which was the method of getting the coal to the yard. A railway truck would be delivered from the colliery just a few miles up the line and the side dropped down, which allowed Roger and his mate to shovel it – yes shovel it – from the truck and onto the yard floor. That was until some clever chap invented a trap door release in the bottom of the truck which revolutionised the whole process.

The work was very hard and whilst Roger looked about sixty, he was only about forty-five. He was, without doubt, the nicest and kindliest of men who looked after his customers, particularly the old people, when coal was scarce and they never forgot that.

To ensure everybody got some coal when it was scarce, he delivered small quantities each week, which must have been uneconomic, but to him, this was the fairest way to keep everybody going. After all, his horse could only deliver so much in a week and that was that.

Apart from Sundays and the Saturday afternoons on which the local football team was at home, Roger was always working. On Sundays, he was a regular churchgoer and a sidesman into the bargain. He invariably had a smile on his face and could always be relied upon to give a helping hand to everyone he met. He had never got around to getting married, but seemed happy at home with his ageing mother, then a widow since losing her husband just before the Second World war. He looked after the heavy housework whilst his mother did the cooking and light shopping. The funny thing about Roger that set him apart from the rest of the neighbourhood, was that I never heard anybody say a bad word about him. He was just a very nice chap in every respect. Unlike so many of the characters described in this missive there isn't a funny or naughty story that I tell about him, but there was an incident that summed up how everyone felt about him, which is well worth relating.

It happened on a winter's day, the time of year when all coal merchants are flat out keeping everybody's coal house topped up. He was delivering down one of the long back streets that divided the rows of houses off our street, when, by accident, he failed to engage the brake on the cart. The horse would normally trundle along at the beckoning of Roger on the releasing of the brake. Too late; the horse set off too quickly and ran over his foot. The weight of the cart plus the load of coal crushed his toes on his left foot. The amazing thing was that he didn't shout or scream like most people would have done, but gently sank to the ground and called for help from a passing lady.

It wasn't until the hospital examined the foot that it became clear that poor old Roger was about to lose several toes as they were beyond treatment. The weight of the cart and the coal combined, plus the steel rimmed wooden wheels, were more than enough for any man and within a day the toes were amputated.

But Roger was no model patient. He constantly badgered the nursing staff about being released. He knew that only he knew the coal round and the consequences of not delivering in the middle of a cold winter. But what was to happen? Well, as my old mother would say: "you reap what you sow in this world" and Roger was about to reap his harvest. As soon as the word spread about the accident, half a dozen able-bodied men turned up at the coal yard and pitched in, filling sacks, loading trucks and sorting out the deliveries with the help of Roger's mate. A rota was formed to keep the deliveries moving and to allow the men to work, as well as helping with the coal. Some people came to collect their coal with wheelbarrows and old prams to help out. It was without doubt a true neighbourly gesture to Roger for all his past good deeds to them.

When he was told what was happening at the yard, he simply broke down and cried in his hospital bed. It was all too much for him. He was always so busy helping others that had never had time for sentiment. He was a doer, but this set-back showed him the other side of life, that people can respond with kindness when it's most needed.

He was up and about in few weeks and insisted on at least driving the cart with his mate doing the rest; much against the wishes of the doctor. But that was Roger all over again. However, this story of Roger had an even happier ending. During his stay in hospital, he met a nurse called Maureen and within six months they were married. His little old mother was over the moon that at last he was settling down. But Roger never forgot those people who rallied round when he was in hospital and convalescing . He hired the parish hall and invited them all to his wedding reception, where he gave a moving speech based on the 'Good Samaritan'. That summed him up really.

Whilst Roger was the good example of a good church-goer, not far away was a somewhat obnoxious religious fanatic who rejoiced in the name of Holy Joe.

Joe was always to be found with his Bible in his hand, spouting the Scriptures to everybody that was within earshot. This included his place of work where he worked on a very large metal shaping machine making ship engine parts.

His machine was directly opposite the heat treatment plant which was worked by a devout Spiritualist called Sam – or Sammy the Spook by his workmates. The two were daggers drawn most of the time despite their religious beliefs, which always had their workmates keen to set up arguments between them.

It was ironical too that Sammy was the shop steward and heavily into Union affairs. This seemed to aggravate Joe even more, especially when the annual pay negotiations came round. He would openly criticise Sammy as the local negotiator for being greedy and caring more for money than people – the old 'God and Mammon' bit. But to make matters worse, Joe was a member of the Union himself, in those days of the 'Closed Shop', and received the benefits of Sammy's negotiating skills, the fact of which Sammy constantly reminded him.

If 'Holy Joe' wanted to ruffle Sammy's feathers he would start singing hymns whilst his machine was performing a long automatic cut on some piece of metal. The 'Spook' would go crazy, banging and clattering anything to hand to try and drown Joe's incredibly bad singing voice. News of the encounter would spread throughout the factory and little columns of blue-clad workers would make their way to the scene of the conflict, whilst not drawing the attention of the Foreman in his office which was up on stilts, giving a panoramic of the factory floor. The only thing that was missing was a machine-gun turret to REALLY keep the workers in check.

Usually, the foreman knew nothing of these encounters which were dubbed the 'Battle of the Crusaders' by the rest of the viewing workforce; a slight overstatement, as this crusade was always about daft subjects that had no bearing on the religious beliefs of either men.

But it seemed that nothing would deter the two from constantly sniping at each other, despite the efforts of their nearby workmates to bring some common-sense to the proceedings.

Matters did however reach a peak during a tea break one day. Whilst Joe and Sammy always had their break as far away as possible from each other, they were still within earshot, which resulted in an argument about religion in general, with everyone around pitching in. The two bigots simply couldn't keep out of the argument, despite the fact that they knew it would end in a shouting match; and it did. But this was serious. They almost came to blows when Joe called Sammy 'Sammy the Spook' a name never used directly to Sammy for fear of the forces of the 'spirits' being brought down or some such twaddle.

It was only the intervention of the foreman, coming down the workshop that brought the proceedings to a halt. There was, however, quite a lot of mumbling and grumbling between the two which went on for the rest of the day. Meanwhile, work continued with Sammy working on the fitting of hot piston rings for very large diesel engines. These rings were about three feet in diameter and had to be suspended above the piston and being very hot, you had to be mighty careful when lowering them onto the piston, which was standing upright.

Joe meanwhile was working on his own machine and singing hymns in a low baritone voice. A shriek pierced the already noisy workshop. It was Sammy. The worst thing possible had happened. The hot ring had somehow been dislodged with Sammy underneath it. The ring in effect spiralled around Sammy burning him as it dropped. Joe, being the First Aid nominee for the workshop, rushed from his machine to Sammy's corner, and, seeing the ring had hit the floor releasing Sammy, pulled him clear. Whilst an ambulance was sent for, it became clear that Sammy was in shock and he fell back unconscious and was having difficulty breathing.

Without a moment's hesitation, Joe started massaging Sammy's heart. But it was clear he was losing ground. This was it: Joe immediately cocked back Sammy's head and gave him mouth to mouth resuscitation. The heat of the moment brought the best out of Joe and all was well. Sammy's breathing was normalised and he lay quietly until the ambulance came and took him to hospital with minor burns and shock.

The funny thing was, that the mouth to mouth method Joe used was very new in this country at the time, and everyone watching wondered what the hell was going on as you can imagine.

Needless to say, Sammy had to thank Joe for his effort on his return home after a few days. Normally this would have been an impossible scene to imagine – Sammy sucking up to Joe.

It wasn't until a tea break sometime afterwards when Sammy returned to work that someone raised the mouth to mouth resuscitation again. Clearly Sammy was not aware Joe had used it on him and when Joe was asked how to do it, who better to ask than Sammy to act as a dummy patient. Sammy recoiled: "You couldn't get me to do that – it's a filthy thing to do."

"I already have – to you!" retorted Joe.

Sammy went white, then grey, then green. He rushed to the nearest door and threw up.

The whole workforce screamed with laughter. What a hoot. Poor old Sammy. He disappeared for a while until he could come to terms with the idea that his somewhat grotty old adversary had more or less kissed him, which was just too much.

When all the laughter had eventually subsided, Joe glibly chimed in, " Hey you," pointing at Sammy, "Remember, you can't pick and choose your patients when they've stopped breathing". How right he was. They never did make it up; the wounds over the years were too deep. Shame really when you think that for that moment when their mouths joined it saved a life. The trouble was that every time Sammy looked at Joe's mouth, usually with a cigarette in it or munching a sandwich very untidily, he nearly threw up.

# CHAPTER 14

Like most young kids, it was quite natural to admire or even worship the older boys or girls at your school or around your neighbourhood. Their exploits were watched eagerly; what they wore or how they combed their hair and so on.

This could often lead to the older boy or girl getting rather big-headed, resulting in people turning off them because of it. This was exactly what happened to the local hero at the top of the school just down our street. He was good at school work, sports, singing with the amateur dramatic group and above all, he was very popular with the girls due to his good looks. His name was Terry. He was fair-haired and very tall for his age and was always smartly dressed . There was a rumour that he spent an hour in front of the mirror just making himself look casual.

Now 'darling Terry' (as he became known, or 'sweety' by those out his earshot as he was a dab hand in the boxing ring) it seemed could do no wrong and to those around who didn't match his many talents, he was, in short, a pain in the arse. So much so, that every time he fell from grace, even with the smallest of things, he would be the subject of sniggering by the rest of the school. But alas, this was so infrequent that it really became so frustrating to the rest, that a plot was hatched to ensnare Terry and knock him off his pedestal for once.

The school sports day was approaching and as usual, Terry would carry off most of the individual boys' events, including the Victor Ludorum trophy for the best overall athlete in the school. Four chaps from his class decided Terry's ego had to be dented once and for all and what better place than the sports field to do it! All the school would be present, including staff and parents, so the audience would be at its biggest to witness Terry's demise.

The sports field comprised a round green circle of grass with the cricket pitch in the middle and a pavilion at one end next to the score board. The football pitches were sprinkled around this centre piece which had the cinder running track all the way around it. The pavilion was, on Sports Day, for the exclusive use of the staff, parents and those senior pupils on duty as programme monitors and refreshment carriers. This latter category was usually delegated to the prettiest girls in their summer school uniforms and who could put forward a decent pair of size 36C bosoms to enhance the proceedings and titillate the school governors, who were invariably men in those days.

The plotters' idea was to get Terry when he was changing at the back of the pavilion and lock him into the storage cupboard under the main area, where everyone was watching the events. Then, when the alarm was raised by him hammering on the door, he would be duly released by some groundsman or other.

But a couple of the plotters had other ideas. They grabbed Terry and stripped off his shirt and shorts and bundled him into the cupboard, totally starkers. But what the plotters had overlooked was that the upper floor was not completely boarded and through sizeable gaps between the planks of wood, you could clearly see through from the bottom AND from the top to the cupboard below!

The plotters lingered before they left Terry in the cupboard glancing upward as if to heaven to see right up dresses of all the school beauties and then they departed, leaving poor Terry with his hands firmly across his privates. He didn't know whether to shout or bang the door of the cupboard, as to do so would almost certainly gain the attention of the people above and he was in no condition to be seen in his state of undress.

Despite his plight, Terry was human too. He too could see up to the next floor and the sight of so much leg and underwear had the inevitable effect on him on that warm summer's day. As things became too difficult for him too handle, (to coin a phrase), Terry became desperate and called as quietly as he could to the plotters outside the door of the cupboard who could see everything through a crack in the door. They were all by now in hysterics and loving every minute of the spectacle. Their humour was difficult to contain and other pupils gathered at the door, pushing and shoving, to get a glimpse of the unfortunate Terry attempting to hold on to his growing problem.

The inevitable happened. An inquisitive tea serving girl on the balcony of the pavilion heard the commotion down below and leant over the rail to see what was going on. Unable to make out why these hoards of marauding youths were clamouring to peer into the cupboard below, she caught a glimpse of the naked youth through the planks on which she was standing, holding something she had only seen in her biology book.

One scream was enough. The Headmaster, being nearby, was quickly on the scene (as were most of the senior girls to see what made Terry tick) and Terry was liberated beneath the jacket of the Head Groundsman to the changing rooms nearby.

Of course, the plot had the opposite effect to its intentions. Terry became more popular than ever; especially with the older girls who recognised his hidden talent even with the restricted view they'd had between the floor boards of the pavilion balcony. More popular too with the girls' gymnastics teacher, who was later dismissed, having been found in the games and activity store (suitably named) with the aforesaid Terry. She proved conclusively that an extra pair of hands was all that Terry needed on that fateful day to cover his modesty and she paid the penalty for being a willing helper. (Or was it a willy helper?)

Whilst covering the indiscretions of the teaching fraternity, several other incidents in a similar vein come to mind at or about the same time. One nearly resulted in a fatal accident. The cast of characters on that occasion were two PE teachers from the nearby senior Church of England school. It resulted in a legal case for assault with the local press making the most of the descriptions of 'who did what to whom' scenario.

The lady in question brought the case of actual assault brought about by an incident that happened after school in the staff room when all others had vacated the premises. She claimed that the man involved had tried to choke her during a 'moment of passion' (and we all knew what that meant) and despite her protests, he pursued some sort of ritual which involved placing a banana in her mouth. The 'offending object', as described in the press, nearly choked her. The reason I knew it was a banana was that my mother said so at the time. I later discovered that it was just one of those things that mothers tell their inquisitive children when they can't bring themselves to tell the truth. Needless to say, every other kid in the school knew what this 'banana incident' was all about, but I didn't believe them either; what was the point of that?

It also seemed a total waste of a good banana, if my mother was right.

As you can see, I didn't know what to believe. Well – I was very young at the time.

The third sexational happening that involved schoolteachers revolved around a local music teacher called Frost. Now Frosty was well known for private piano teaching with a difference. He didn't discriminate between boys or girls when pursuing his lecherous ways and apparently spent most of the time with his hands where they shouldn't be. I suppose nowadays he would be headline news, but there was a certain code that nobody 'ratted' on people like Frosty, but simply withdrew their children at the first hint of trouble.

Frosty wasn't married but had a very catholic taste in personal relationships. He seemed to dominate the lives of one particular set of sisters; there were three of them. We used to call them 'Grace, Disgrace and Candlegrace'. They would be constantly harassing each other as to who would be going up to

Frosty's house to do his washing etc. Neither of these three, nor Frosty for that matter, was married and were, to say the least, in the twilight of their years. What the attraction was we will never know, but it went on for years. But none of the 'Three Graces' was allowed to be at Frosty's house during his teaching sessions. We all knew why too!

It wasn't until one enterprising girl – much fancied by all the boys – decided enough was enough. This came to light when Frosty was seen trying unsuccessfully to hide a plaster cast on his hand and wrist. Apparently this voluptuous young thing was playing away on the piano with Frosty's hands roaming around, when she persuaded him to show her the fingering of one piece of music. Wham! She slammed down the lid onto his fingers and off to hospital he went.

The 'Three Graces' put it about that Frosty had trapped his hand in a slamming door, but we all knew differently. He was more likely to get it trapped in slamming thighs. He died a rather nasty death did old Frosty. Killed in a road accident taking a pupil to an examination – the pupil survived. Apparently he lost control of the vehicle and crashed into a wall. Rumours were abroad that he had not got both hands on the steering wheel at the time. Well – that was Frosty – always trying to get a grip on the situation.

# CHAPTER 15

"Anything to get you lot out of the house", the eternal cry of mothers during school holidays, was often heard down and around our street.

"Will you not get out from under my feet?" was another plea when things were really bad. This was particularly apt when it was raining and all of us kids were stuck in the house and causing trouble.

At about that time, just after the war and school holidays were well underway, a bright spark by the name of Arnold, or Arnie to his mates, hit on the idea of the latest craze of train-spotting.

"Just think," said Arnie, "We can stand by the railway lines near the station and spot trains all day without me mother gettin' on to us". We all thought it was a brilliant idea and started by getting our mothers to cough up two bob to buy the train-spotter's guide. This marvellous book had all the names and details of every train (it really should be engine spotting) in the country, complete with all the technical details and grades of engines. The idea was simply to spot one of these great feats of engineering huffing and puffing and coming your way; make a note of its name or number and cross it out of your book. When you had successfully completed all the sections, you could start all over again. Sounds, when put like that, very boring, but it never was to us lads, eager to fill up the pages with lines indicating what you had seen and proudly showing your mates.

The truth is that very few people completed the whole book, as engines were often based in their own region and hardly ever seen outside it. This meant that for a special day out you would have to travel to other towns such as York or Darlington to broaden your range of spotting. Now this was all very radical and often mothers were torn between letting you go on a trip or having you around the house and causing problems.

Arnie was dead keen on a trip to Darlington and arranged for several of the lads to get a train there as early as possible one holiday morning. All turned up with their macks and A picnic, which consisted of a boiled egg, a corned beef sandwich and an apple. For those with exclusive tastes, a jam sandwich was added to complete the fare and of course, the inevitable bottle of water. In those days before soft drinks were easily available and drinking water not easy to find, it was always prudent to bring your own. Sounds crazy nowadays, but it was true nevertheless.

Arnie's enthusiasm for the day's 'spotting' was always the driving force for the rest of the party. With his immaculate spotter's guide he could recall the day when each entry of trains spotted was seen, and who he was with and how they had nearly seen the Sir Nigel Gresly at the same spot, only to be thwarted by a passing goods train that blocked the view. It was rip roaring stuff and no mistake.

On arrival at Darlington, there was major setback. The small party was removed from the station platform which was the best possible vantage point in this huge station. The station master had decreed it, since some boy had fooled about and fallen onto the track. Luckily, nothing was coming, but that was that. No more 'spotters' on the platform. A porter suggested that the lads made their way to an embankment overlooking the engine sheds and main line to London. Bingo! The place was teeming with named engines of every class. Arnie nearly fell down the embankment with excitement. Page after page was being filled up and appetites seemed to fade so much so, that the picnic was almost forgotten. Then suddenly the noise every train-spotter dreams of: "STREAK!" went up the cry. The wonderful sound of one of the rare breed of engine with its almost strangled scream that could be heard miles away, which gave everybody a chance to get into position. Then gradually it came into view, it's blue side cowling unmistakable and its curved front and stubby funnel only a few inches high. But the name, what was the damn name! The eyes of all the 'spotters' were straining in the direction of the name plate "IT'S MALLARD! IT'S MALLARD! IT'S BLOODY MALLARD!" shrieked Arnie; and it was.

The fastest steam train in the world. It held the record then for the fastest haul of all time – 240 tons at 120 miles per hour from Edinburgh to London. It sped by, that wonderful, beautiful, graceful beast, shrieking as it went and quickly disappeared leaving a trail of smoke that filled the nostrils like some oriental drug. Then silence. Nobody spoke. It was a moment of complete joy and fulfilment for the 'spotters'. Arnie, everyone said afterwards, was reduced to tears of sheer joy.

"It really was her – bloody Mallard" he was just coming round, like somebody speaking after an operation, slowly and dreamily. He quietly opened his carrier bag containing his picnic and munched his corned beef sandwich, interspersed with slugs of water. He said nothing more so everybody followed suit and munched away at their picnics.

It was about time to go anyway, as their train back home was due in half an hour. They slowly made their way back to the station were they saw the porter who had told them where to get the best views of the trains and engines in the sheds nearby. Arnie mumbled a "Thanks very much – we saw Mallard". The train journey home was still subdued, but on arrival at our home station, Arnie saw some of his mates by the entry gates. He couldn't wait to let rip with the full details of the great Mallard and the exploits of the day. The gathering throng were open mouthed. "Hey, have you 'erd? Arnie and the lads saw the Mallard!" They passed the message around the other spotters nearby.

It truly was a red letter day for this little band of 'spotters'. They all slept soundly that night, going to bed without the usual argy-bargy with mother.

"What's come over you son – you're very quiet" Arnie's mother said with a querying voice when he arrived home.

"I saw Mallard today mam," said Arnie with a vacant look on his face."

That's nice son, but I thought you went train-spottin'?" she replied.

"We did," retorted Arnie a little irritated.   She looked somewhat puzzled at him, paused and said –

"But I thought a Mallard was a duck?"


Near our home town railway station was the locally famous Railway Canteen.   It was a venue for rough and ready meals served at a fast pace.   Despite its title, it was open to the public and well patronised.   It was in direct competition with the British Restaurant mentioned earlier and indeed the competition was very severe.

Regularly each of these houses of very indifferent food would spy on each others menus chalked on a blackboard outside, which was required then by local by-laws.   Quick alterations were not unknown to entice the public indoors, particularly if one or the other had managed to get some unusual dish ingredients in those days of scarcity.   The press got hold of this competitive activity and would regularly publish the skirmishes of price reductions of the Bread and Butter Pudding or Spotted Dick.   The arrival of the very first banana brought fear to the Railway Canteen and Restaurant; yes, they even changed the name to attract more up-market customers, as the British Restaurant had secured the first bulk consignment in the town.   'Traditional Banana Pudding', and 'Caribbean Banana Split with REAL Ice Cream' was chalked up proudly on the British Restaurant menu board.

This was all too much for the 'Railway', as it was usually known; they had to do something and pretty fast.

Now it was usual when attending these fast food type establishments that you brought your own cutlery with you.   A real post-war problem was the lack of steel for household implements and such establishments simply couldn't kit the place out fully so you normally brought your own to avoid the hire charge.

The 'Railway' decided to put the British Restaurant's bananas out of business and introduced knives, forks and spoons at every table FREE OF CHARGE. This was real warfare. How they did it was a closely guarded secret, but stamp markings on the back had clearly been filed away, but the imprint of 'BR' could still be seen on some. One had the picture of some express train's restaurant car hurtling along with the passengers eating the food with their fingers on discovering the cutlery missing.

However, all was not as it seemed (rather like the food) at the 'Railway'. They had informed the press about their tableware gimmick who ran a story after a visit. Alas, the reporter rushed back with an even better story. Sure, the knives, forks and spoons were there but were very firmly screwed to the table via a chain at every position and washed in a travelling bucket after each customer had left.

The headline in the evening paper read: 'HOW TO SCREW DOWN THE OPPOSITION'.

It was the intervention of the Health Inspector that stopped the rewashing of the cutlery at the table and the experiment collapsed. The headline followed 'THE RAILWAY FINED AFTER SCREWING PROBE' – mmm!

# CHAPTER 16

Stories from the many factories around our street were legion. Some were funny; some were tragic; but they typify the nature of the times when most people had a job and everybody seemed to know their place. Here are a few yarns that improve with the telling.

It was the 'custom', that in most of the engineering factories it was relatively easy to get someone to make you a fireside shovel or a poker, during the time they should have been working of course, in return for a few bob or a packet or two of cigarettes. Now making these tools when the Foreman wasn't looking was one thing, but smuggling them out of the factory gates was another.

Highly coloured fireside pokers were a speciality. Beautifully finished with a high polish ensured a good reward. No matter how they tried, the management could not stamp out this practice despite threats of the sack or suspension.

Then came one of those painful experiences that everybody who made these tools dreaded. At the end of the day's work the whole mass of the workforce would leave together. Most people on foot or on bikes filed passed the gate with the security guard looking for anything that looked suspicious. The exit was on a slope and was made of cobble stones and with the heavy footwear of the workers, it was quite noisy. Then 'CLANG CLANG': a metal object had hit the ground. Somebody had dropped a poker with the most beautifully coloured handle and it was rolling very gently down the slope of cobblestones towards he exit gate.

Nobody looked down, gestured, cried out – nothing. Everybody continued as if nothing had happened. The poker steadily rolled towards the feet of the security guard who nonchalantly bent down and picked it up and addressed the exiting throng: "This anybody's?" he shouted, holding it up.

Nobody even flickered. The mass exodus continued as if nothing had happened. Someone in the throng was wincing internally that weeks of work were down the tube with nothing to show for it. It was all the more galling when it was later discovered that the security guard was seen selling it in the local pub the next day. There's no justice.

One thing that was a worry in those factories that made large steel vessels, was a fire breaking out during construction. Some of these vessels were up to fifty feet high and, if a fire broke out, usually from a welder's torch, all hell was let loose.

One particular apprentice by the name of Bertram (he was one of the boss's sons put into an apprenticeship to 'blood' him before stepping into a management job) was paranoid about fires. Most of the time he started them with piles of rubbish he had gathered and regularly had to be taken to task by the foreman. He was simply a pyromaniac.

This was a constant source of irritation to the rest of the workforce, who found it difficult to tackle the boss's son, without getting an earful from the foreman relating to "exceeding your authority".

This had all gone too far for one bold journeyman by the name of Tom Nutt. Recently back from National Service, he did not appreciate the antics of Bertram nor his position in the hierarchy and promptly set about to fix him.

As luck would have it, Bertram had been seconded to work with Tom in one of those very large steel vessels being made for the Electricity Board, fitting it out with all manner of compartments and ladders. Tom picked his moment. With Bertram halfway up the vessel, fixing brackets to the side, Tom lit a small bunch of rags at the bottom of the vessel, which was some thirty feet high. "Fire!" shouted Tom, with all his might.

Bertram was frantic. But instead of scuttling down to the bottom of the vessel where another apprentice was waiting with a fire hose poised to blast at Bertram legitimately, he ran as fast as he could to an escape ladder which was fixed to the side of the vessel. Alas, he had overlooked one very significant point – the ladder was incomplete and stopped halfway up. Bertram was going nowhere!

As Bertram had not appeared at the bottom, Tom peered into the vessel through a manhole where he espied the stranded Bertram. "Help get me down!" pleaded the hapless Bertram.

Tom obliged with a ladder, but not before the apprentice with the hose was quietly instructed to give Bertram a dousing for good measure, on the understanding that he was trying to put out the fire.

News of this 'ladder escape to nowhere' quickly spread and Bertram got a special cheer when he entered the works canteen at lunchtime.

"Hey up Bertie Boy! What about a repeat of the 'The ladder to nowhere'?" came the cry from some erstwhile wag munching his bread and butter pudding.

"Wait till your Old Man hears about it cocker! He'll have you on permanent fire drill!" came another.

Bertram was so furious that he hadn't noticed that someone ahead of him in the queue had spilled a portion of custard on the floor. Crash! Bang! Wallop! Down went Bertram, tray, lunch and all.

Tom was passing at that moment and bent over the hapless Bertram: "I should stick to ladders if I were you my lad," said Tom.

Bertram had learned his lesson: well, nearly. He was missing for some time the following day and the foreman had a message for him from his 'Pater'. Unable to find him, he inquired of another apprentice as to his whereabouts. The youth advised him that he was last seen at the gatehouse some time ago. Anxious to locate him, the foreman went to the gatehouse and there he was, just standing there with his hands in his pockets.

"What's to do young Bertram?" said the bewildered foreman." What are you doing here?"

"Oh well sir, I have been sent here to collect a stand" said Bertram.

"What sort of a stand?" enquired the foreman.

"A long one sir," replied Bertram.

"Precisely what was the request, young man?" asked the foreman, smelling a distinct 'rat'.

" Well sir, my journeyman told me go to the gatehouse for a long stand and the man at the desk said to wait here," said a pleading Bertram.

"You've been 'had' son," said the resolute foreman. "Now get back to your job."

The foreman shook his head at the man at the desk who replied by shrugging his shoulders. Bertram quickly learned that although he was the boss's son, he was no different to any other apprentice. They had all been 'had' at some time which was all part the scene. I often wonder if he told his Dad?

After his workshop apprenticeship, Bertram was seconded to the Drawing Office as part of his training for management. It was during this period that he became very involved with sports cars, mostly the open top variety. He dabbled in collecting old clapped out cars and refurbishing them and if he found a buyer, he would sell them at a handsome profit.

All this activity meant that he appeared at the office in different cars, boring everybody stiff with his exploits as to how he bought them and what he was going to do with them. This often got up the noses of the staff, most of whom were poorly paid, as they could not hope to run a car, let alone buy one. It was the push bike or the bus for most of them and Bertram's affluence was all too much for them to take and the inevitable happened.

Having been ranting on about the latest MG sports car he had just bought, complete with drop hood and spoked wheels, two or three other draughtsmen set about to fix Bertram and teach him a lesson.

To achieve their mission, Bertram would have to be out of the way for about an hour and, as a training film was being shown in the canteen, Bertram was enlisted and was to be away from the office for about two hours on that day. Perfect. The appointed hour came and the innocent Bertram toddled off to the canteen and the training film.

As it was the afternoon, by the time Bertram returned to the drawing office it was time to go home. As usual he cleared his desk, donned his leather driving coat, hat, goggles and gloves and proceeded to the car park, hotly pursued by all of the staff at a great distance to avoid being too obvious.

On approaching his parking slot, he stopped in his tracks – the car clearly was not there. He walked slowly up and down the row of managers' cars and back again. Nothing.

He untied his goggles and stripped off his gloves and looked around for someone to ask about the whereabouts of his pride and joy. It wasn't until the office clerk, a spotty-faced individual called Morton or Morty to all of the staff, came out of the office and was mounting his bike, that Bertram could get any clues as to the location of his car.

Morty gave a wry smile and said: "Just look up."

Bertram was totally bemused. "Look up? What the hell do you mean?" said the even more frustrated Bertram.

But look up he did, as Morty cycled away, and, to his horror, there was his pride and joy! Not as he expected, but on the top compartment of the adjacent pipe rack, neatly parked about fifteen feet above ground in one of the giant pipe slots. But that was not all. The perpetrators of this dastardly act had welded across the face of the rack a large piece of steel, totally imprisoning the car. This was desperate stuff.

It would not be difficult for anyone reading this tale to add the expletives that Bertram uttered at that incredible moment, so I won't bother. Suffice it to say, that to my young ears at the time I quickly added to my vocabulary numerous ones of a very descriptive nature, mostly centring around sex and travel.

Poor old Bertram – as there was nothing he could do, he hitched a lift home with a colleague. To his eternal credit, he did not let his father know of this prank, as the consequences would have been dire. He simply dropped a few pounds to a friendly welder after hours the next day who cut the car free and lowered it via the gib to safety. He never found out who did it, but from then onwards, he was very careful about his somewhat affluent lifestyle being banded around the drawing office and he was better off for it.

He never did become a manager after all the careful training, but finished up putting one of the girls from the factory football team in the family way and emigrating to Australia. The girl was left behind to have the baby, which was adopted and taken out of the area.

Within a few years the factory closed, drawing office and all, and Bertram, his father and all the rest were just history. That's life.

# CHAPTER 17

One of the highlights of the year for everyone living and working around our street was the visit of the circus, with the wonderful side shows that to most of us kids was far better than the circus itself.

Much to the annoyance of the local sports fraternity, the whole show was housed for the week's visit, on the local recreation ground. This resulted in the football pitches being ploughed up by the huge wagons which carried all the gear and, of course, the animals.

Part of the circus would arrive by train and parade through the town with all the elephants and horses leading the clowns and acrobats. This would always cause a stir, as the elephants would inevitably leave a trail of dung behind in huge mounds which was quickly scooped up by the keen local gardeners. We kids would roar with delight when an elephant would oblige and run away from the heap holding our noses.

But it was the sideshows that caught the imagination of us kids. This comprised a number of marquees and wagons, with notices outside that made the eyes of wondering kids, fairly pop out.

'The Amazing Bearded Lady', 'The Fattest Woman On Earth', 'The Tallest Man on Earth', 'The World's Only Surviving Siamese Twins', 'The Famous Flea Circus', and my favourite: 'The Smallest Woman on Earth'.

What a feast of weird spectacles they were! No child, or adult for that matter, could resist an evening of sheer wonderment gawping at these most unusual creatures.

But the 'Smallest Woman on Earth' sticks vividly in my mind. Entering her marquee, we were confronted by what appeared at first glance to be an oversized doll's house with the walls opened up. It had furniture made in bright colours with chandeliers hanging down making a dazzling scene of a palacelike room, but much smaller. Then from behind the curtains came the strangest form of humanity that I have ever seen in my whole life to this day. A perfectly formed doll-like female emerged wearing a silver, twenties style, tight-fitting evening dress that went to floor level. You could have been forgiven for thinking that it a was wind-up doll; but it wasn't. It was a real live person, with long hair tied loosely at the back and smoking a cigarette from a miniature cigarette holder. The only difference was that she was no more than two feet high!

There was absolute silence in the marquee, as we slowly wound around the rope barriers, all eyes absolutely transfixed on this amazing person: so small, but perfect in every other way. It was a sight I will never forget. The silence was only interspersed by a minute crackling voice which said 'Keep moving along please'. It was even more incredible when I realised that it was this tiny creature speaking, whilst she promenaded from one side of the stage to the other, occasionally sitting and then standing. This we all supposed afterwards was to make absolutely sure that all present realised that she was real and not some sort of artificial doll. On leaving the marquee, hardly anyone spoke as we were so shocked by what we had seen.

The other shows came and went but the little lady, so elegant yet so small, stopped the show: well, nearly.

The final night of this week of travelling weirdos, was capped by the incomparable high diving routine, known throughout the land as 'Powsey's Last Dive'. This incredible one-armed man would, once per day, dive into a water tank which was blazing with lighted fuel from a height of about two hundred feet.

But on Saturday night, the last night of the show, he would dive whilst on fire himself and through a hoop which was also on fire! The publicity for this event read 'Powsey's Last Dive – ON FIRE – THROUGH FIRE – AND INTO FIRE'.

The crowds gathered in their hundreds to witness this incredible feat of courage, because laying all the hype aside, it was extremely dangerous. It was dusk by the time the actual event took place, which made the whole spectacle of fire-diving a real and awesome sight. Eventually, Powsey appeared, dressed in a leotard and cape which had his name emblazoned on it, showing huge flames shooting up from the water tank with a Superman style figure diving head first from the high tower. It was all great stuff for us kids, being out late at night, amongst this huge crowd which was growing by the minute. With a fanfare of trumpets screaming out of the loudspeakers, Powsey started his ascent of the narrow ladder, with a trail of searchlights following him all the way up, until he was a tiny figure almost too far up to see in detail. His left arm had been severed at the elbow which we were told, was as a direct result of a past dive going wrong. The speculation was rife. Would it go wrong tonight again? The tension was unbearable. He seemed to be struggling to lift himself from rung to rung, but at last he reached the top. He turned triumphantly to acknowledge the crowd far below.

We could just see him removing his cape which he fixed to a rope and lowered to the ground. He faced a giant ring which was hardly distinguishable against the sky which by now was quite black. There was a pause and an announcement came over loudspeakers "This is Powsey's last dive, ladies and gentlemen, please give generously". At that point, several huge chaps were pushing their way through the crowd with collection buckets. They looked so menacing that people automatically reached into their pockets and dropped the coins into the buckets as they passed.

From high on the diving platform, Powsey gave the signal to the attendants below and the huge steel tank towering above us kids was set alight. With a 'whoosh', the flames spread across the tank. All eyes were set on Powsey. A small light could be seen at the top of the platform and within a second the huge ring was alight, followed by the flames extending to Powsey himself and in flash he dived off. This flaming object was hurtling to the towards the tank. Would he hit it? The crowd gasped. The biggest splash you ever saw lurched from the tank. The flames went out immediately as if by a miracle. The water was still swirling and splashing over the side of the tank. But where was Powsey? An agonising few seconds which seemed liked hours passed before an arm - well, half an arm - reached over the side followed quickly by a second. Powsey pulled himself over the edge helped by his assistants. He was covered in oily water, but it made no matter. The crowd roared. He was helped to the floor and immediately handed a bucket and proceeded to collect from the crowd.

He was cheered and cheered and noise of coins hitting the bucket will always stick in my memory as he made his way through the crowd to his caravan. It was all heady stuff. But most of all, it was REAL. He actually did dive two hundred feet on fire, through fire and into fire. Powsey was a hero, and we loved it and went home to bed exhausted with tension and took no time in falling fast asleep.


As with all such great moments, something tragically humorous can often arise and this was no exception. About three doors from the barber's shop down our street lived a slightly simple lad called Willie Brown. Alas, Willie was born not quite right in the head and never went to school, but lived a simple life with his ageing parents without causing difficulties for anyone.

The Powsey dive, however, had been seen by Willie and had clearly had an effect on him. Egged on by some daft kids, Willie decided to do his own dive unknown to his parents. He filled a metal bath with water and from the garden fence dived head first into it. He never recovered consciousness and died several days later. His parents were distraught and within two years, both had died, presumably from the delayed shock. Kids can be cruel and for years afterwards they told the story of

'Willie's last Dive', long after Powsey was forgotten. Life's like that.


These yarns from down our street could not be complete without a couple more tales from around the church we all attended. The first revolves around the visit to the parish one Sunday evening by local Archdeacon Drum. Better known throughout the diocese as Kit. (No, there are no prizes for guessing why.)

Now Kit was a war hero and had suffered the loss of his lower right leg as a result of a land mine in the First World War. He was, however, still very active and whilst climbing the pulpit steps was always a slow business, he had mastered the motor car and was often seen roaring about the parishes in his converted Austin Seven.

The day in question, Kit was due to preach at our local Harvest Festival and had arranged to arrive for tea with our vicar at about four o'clock. Never having been late before, when four-fifteen struck, the vicar became worried when Kit had not appeared. By four-thirty, the vicar could wait no longer and telephoned his home.

Even more worryingly, they had waved him off over an hour earlier and had heard nothing since. The vicar immediately rang the police – but there was no news there either and apart from promising to search for Kit, there was nothing much they could do. So, everybody simply had to wait by the telephone.

At about five-thirty the phone rang – it was Kit's wife. She said all was well, but he would be a little late and could we hold Evensong until he arrived and that Kit would explain about the delay on his arrival.

Well, as Evensong was late by about ten minutes when he drove up in his car, there was no time for explanations and in they went.

Kit, forever the humorist, could not keep his reason for his late arrival to himself and decided to preamble his sermon with the story. Apparently he 'took short', as they say, on his way to our Evensong and had to make an emergency stop at a public bar he was passing. Having pulled into the car park at the rear, he made his way to the toilet and excused himself to the publican on the way.

On his way back to his car, he caught the foot of his artificial leg in a drain and tripped very heavily. That was bad enough, but in doing so, his artificial leg snapped off and bounced some yards away. Not fancying a commando crawl across the car park, he managed to open the door of the car and get on the seat. But that was all he could do. Without his other leg he was going nowhere. There was nothing for it but to sound the horn to attract someone from the bar to rescue him. It wasn't until a rather inebriated chap, being considerably the worse for drink, emerged from the back of the bar.

Kit immediately sounded the horn and shouted across that he needed help.

At this point, the congregation listening to this story started to giggle.

"Imagine the scene" said Kit. "A clergyman sitting in the back car park of a bar in the middle of nowhere on a Sunday afternoon, seeking the assistance of a rather drunken man, who staggered up to the car in which he was sitting and asking him to kindly fetch him his leg, which was some yards away."

The congregation by this time were in hysterics. Kit went on in measured tones, as if announcing the start of World war Three.

"The somewhat puzzled inebriate then when he had stopped laughing, and convinced that I had indeed lost my leg, once in the war and now in this pub car park on a Harvest Festival Sunday afternoon, decided he would get help."

In true Churchillian style, Kit continued.

"Now imagine the inebriate re-entering the pub and starting to explain to the gathered throng, being equally drunk, about my predicament in the car park. Indeed, it wasn't for some minutes that the landlord, accompanied by this chap, came to my car to verify the situation. Indeed, it wasn't until I had actually shown him my absent leg and my artificial one some yards away, that he actually believed me."

Suffice to say, the leg was returned, albeit broken, which resulted in his reserve one being sent for which caused most of the delay. The message of the harvest being gathered in safely was never more vividly portrayed that evening to a congregation still aching with laughter from this story.

# CHAPTER 18

The days before motor cars were seen at every door, the occasional day trips by coach to the country and towns outside our area, were always a treat.

I was lucky enough to have an active grandmother who loved travelling and always took me along for company on those coach trips.

Mostly they were all female outings that tolerated a small person like me being stuffed in the corner of the back seat, thus avoiding having to pay full fare or any fare at all, if my gran had any say in the matter.

She was an amazing woman; full of energy despite being wracked with asthma which eventually shortened her life at the tender age of sixty-two. As soon as she had 'wind' (as she would put it) of an impending trip being organised around our street, she was on to it in a flash. Despite hardly having two shillings to rub together, she loved a day out on the coach. I suppose it was a respite from the daily grind, plus the chance of escaping from the dreadful atmosphere that was thrown up daily from the nearby steelworks.

The trips to the races were her special favourite. I don't suppose that the bookies at these race-courses were thrilled by the level of betting – usually six pence each way if they were lucky. I mean six old pence to new readers, referred to as a 'tanner each way' by Gran who, it must be said, probably set off with no more than a pound in her pocket to see out the day.

But off we went, bright and early in those pre-motorway days, when a trip to York races was all of two to three hours. Today it would be half that. On scrambling into the coach, you were invariably confronted by a lady handing out song sheets! The idea of singing at that early hour – usually about 7.30am – to allow for traffic and numerous stops for ablutions and the more popular stops for 'refreshments', was daft. Now these 'refreshments' took the form of stopping at every pub on the way that could accommodate a coach. Well that is what it seemed like to me from my angle. The remainder of the trip was interspersed with bottles of milk stout being handed around from the 'kitty', i.e., part of the fare, from crates stuffed under the seats and reserve supplies in the rear hold of the coach.

As the journey progressed, the song sheet was well and truly thumbed with all the old favourites, 'Daisy, Daisy', 'It's a long way to Tipperary', 'Comrades', and the like. All songs that were used to be played and sung at the old music halls, mostly fireside songs that everybody in those days would automatically join in. There was no shyness it seemed to me – they just pitched in – voice or no voice.

Looking back now, as an adult for a moment, 'the stay at home' culture started in the Sixties when the advent of television stopped all that. But as these carefree souls, who between them had never seen a television in those post-war days, set about singing these old favourites, I snuggled down beside my gran and took it all in.

There were some very enterprising women organisers of these trips who not only included old songs, but set about writing their own, mainly of a rather naughty vintage.

Now, as a youngster, this really caught my attention as anything that had the smell of naughtiness or mentioned various parts of the body that were out of sight, was of considerable interest. These songs, however, only came out when the travelling throng of cackling females (and me) had experienced sufficient stops for 'refreshments'. Or that the reserve supplies in the boot had been raided to a level where the atmosphere in the coach was virtually 100% alcohol.

I remember one song to this day, which was a parody of a Jewish song, and with apologies in advance to all my Jewish friends, it went like this:-

Three Jews went to Jerusalem
Three Jews went to Jerusalem
Jerry Jerry Jerry ru salem
Jerry Jerry Jerry ru salem
They all went to Jerusalem

They all fell over a precipice
They all fell over a precipice
Preci Preci Preci – piss piss piss
Preci Preci Preci – piss piss piss
They all fell over a precipice

(you can see how it's going!)

They all went to the hospital
They all went to the hospital
Hossi Hossi Hossi – pital pital pital
Hossi Hossi Hossi – pital pital pital
They all went to the hospital

They washed themselves in carbollick

I will leave the rest for you to work out for yourselves.
Now, to today, that would not have caused much of a stir, but
in those days that was really naughty. My Gran would be on
the edge of a seizure with laughing at these and other far more
risqué songs that occupied the time on these long journeys.

It has been said that all female occasions like this are worse
than men for plumbing the depths of depravity and having seen
both, these trips tended to endorse that theory. But it was still a
lot of fun just watching grown-ups acting like children for a
while. It really was very harmless.

The facilities at racecourses in those days left a lot to be
desired, especially the lavatories. Both male and females had to
make do with sheets of marquee-type cloth made up as a pen –
rather like sheep – which people of all types who could not

afford to pay for an enclosure ticket, had to use. The only concession was that the male and female 'enclosures' were at least separate.

It wasn't until one day at Ripon Races on a bank holiday, when a very strong wind blew up and flattened the female lavatory enclosure. This was a sight to behold. Females in various stages of undress were screaming as the whole crowd witnessed their predicament. I thought it was a hoot, but I was very young at the time.

There were, on these trips, two old ladies who were very hard of hearing from the local chapel. They were usually included when we visited picturesque places or other seaside resorts, as it was generally assumed that they could not bear the bawdy songs or jokes. However, on one such trip during a quiet moment in the journey, they were overheard by the whole coach discussing the new pastor at the chapel. As they were quite hard of hearing, they spoke very loudly and the conversation went something like this:

"Have you met the new pastor yet?"

"Oh yes" – (smugly) – "he's very nice but he does shout."

"He does what?"

"Shout."

"What's that?"

"SHOUT – BAWLS LIKE A BULL!"

"Has he?"

My education was complete.

Reflecting on those far off days as a young lad, the people round and about our street WERE the street. The community was a real unit, but with many separate parts contributing to the whole. Your neighbours were your friends, sharing the ups and downs of life. Births, marriages and deaths involved everybody and you expected nothing else. This closeness was all too apparent during the war years which spilled over into a post-war period of further shortages of virtually everything.

Somehow we made the best of it, despite shops with nothing on the shelves save a few tins of spam or corned beef. The stories and happenings form an endless stream of memories; some happy some sad, but always full of basic humanity and genuineness. Now half a century later, they are as vivid as when they occurred, probably because it was such an integral part of a very simple life with few distractions, which made our street so special. Whatever it was, I'm not complaining; it was a well established college in that often quoted 'University of Life', from whence so much endeavour was exercised, in those attempts to escape to a better life.

Our street doesn't exist now. They pulled most of it down to build the inevitable by-pass. It seemed the only reason for doing it was because every other town had one, as the traffic is very hard to find most of the time.

Whilst my own house has gone, the one and only tree, a cherry blossom, remains. On standing near it, I can see the shapes of the way things were in my mind's eye; the ghosts of those incredible characters, larger than life in those days, but now gone for ever. Well not quite. Their antics form an indelible part of my memory which, thank God, can never be erased.